Praise for
The 17 Indisputable Laws of Teamwork

Dr. Maxwell, a proven expert on leadersh great leader must rely on others to create *Laws of Teamwork*, the complexities of teamw meaningful process for building and empow

—*... ...er, Alticor*
Owner and Ch... ...n, NBA Orlando Magic

The 17 laws are all true. I have seen their proof in the teams I've coached, and John has done a remarkable job of distilling them into individual, meaningful, teachable principles. Just start with one or two—soon, you'll be applying all 17 of the laws of teamwork, once you see the effect they can have on your own team.

—*Pat Head Summitt*
Women's Basketball Coach, University of Tennessee, Knoxville

You will find this book indispensable whether your team is your family, your business, or your ball club. Maxwell's laws are timeless. No matter what kind of team you're building, this book can help you. Maxwell really knows his stuff!

—*Chris Mortensen*
ESPN Commentator

John Maxwell, America's leadership coach, has done it again. Only this time the subject is teamwork. John's new book is the definitive analysis of teamwork. You've got to read it and then spread the word.

—*Pat Williams*
Sr. Vice President of the Orlando Magic

I have had the privilege of taking players to the highest level in my sport, so I know what it takes to build a championship team. In his latest book, John Maxwell brings the same keen insight to the subject of teamwork that he did to leadership in his previous book. I wholeheartedly recommend *The 17 Indisputable Laws of Teamwork*.

—*Dan Reeves*
Head Coach, The Atlanta Falcons

John Maxwell personifies effective leadership. He is both talented and learned. In *The 17 Indisputable Laws of Teamwork* he shares his analytical scholarship, illustrated with real-life situations.

—Fred Smith, Sr.
Contributing Editor, Leadership Today

An entrepreneur needs Maxwell's book to create the team to give his life to the dream.

—Lowell W. Paxson,
Chairman Paxson Communications Corporation
PAX TV

John Maxwell has done it again. Here is a book about teamwork that is insightful and stuffed full of memorable anecdotes, creative illustrations, and down-to-earth, practical advice. I thoroughly enjoyed it and you will too!

—Pat MacMillan
CEO, Team Resources, INC.
Atlanta, GA

I really enjoyed reading *The 17 Indisputable Laws of Teamwork.* It fits very much in my philosophy.

—Bobby Bowden
Head Football Coach
Florida State University

Having coached high school football teams and then having built a business team from 85 agents to 225,000 at A. L. Williams, I applaud John Maxwell for *The 17 Indisputable Laws of Teamwork.* I would recommend this book to any leader, no matter how large or small their team may be. Everyone still loves a winner and this book is full of proven winners.

—Art Williams
Founder A. L. Williams

Individuals score points, but teams win games. In *The 17 Indisputable Laws of Teamwork,* individuals will learn how to score more points so their teams will win more games.

—Zig Ziglar
Author/Motivational Teacher

THE 17 INDISPUTABLE LAWS OF TEAMWORK

Embrace Them and Empower Your Team

JOHN C. MAXWELL

NELSON BOOKS
A Division of Thomas Nelson Publishers
Since 1798

www.thomasnelson.com

Published in Nashville, Tennessee, by Thomas Nelson, Inc.

Scripture quotations noted KJV are from the KING JAMES VERSION.

ISBN 978-973-99872-4-0

Library of Congress Control Number 2001 132671

Printed in Belarus, 2007

This book is dedicated
to the people of The INJOY Group:

You make me better than I am.
You multiply my value to others.
You enable me to do what I do best.
You give me more time.
You represent me where I cannot go.
You provide community for my enjoyment.
You fulfill the desires of my heart.
I can never thank you enough!

About the Companion Web Site

To enhance and complete your teamwork learning experience, we invite you to visit our companion Web site at www.LawsOfTeamwork.com.

Read *The 17 Indisputable Laws of Teamwork.*

Apply what you learn by following the suggestions at the end of each chapter.

Log on at the free interactive assessment developed by The INJOY Group. It will help you gauge your strengths and weaknesses when it comes to teamwork. There you will also find recommendations for ways to further your personal and professional development.

We hope you enjoy the book and the Web site, and we trust that you will embrace the Laws of Teamwork and empower your team.

Thomas Nelson Publishers and The INJOY Group

CONTENTS

ACKNOWLEDGMENTS

Every book I write is an act of teamwork. And this one is no exception. I'd like to thank the people who helped me to create *The 17 Indisputable Laws of Teamwork:*

The INJOY Team, who helped me to think through and refine the laws.

Margaret Maxwell, my wife, best friend, and number one teammate, who gives good advice.

Linda Eggers, who always takes care of all the details of my life.

Kathie Wheat, who did such wonderful research for the book.

Stephanie Wetzel, who sharpened the manuscript by proofreading and editing every word.

Charlie Wetzel, whose writing extends my influence around the world.

INTRODUCTION

Every day, in some way, you are a part of a team. The question is not, *Will you participate in something that involves others?* The question is, *Will your involvement with others be successful?* You can find the answer to that question in this book.

Everyone knows that teamwork is a good thing; in fact, it's essential! But how does it really work? What makes a winning team? Why do some teams go straight to the top, seeing their vision become reality, while others seem to go nowhere?

These questions don't have simple answers. If they did, sports would have more back-to-back world champions, and the list of Fortune 500 companies would never change year after year.

One of the challenges of learning about teamwork is that even people who've taken a team to the highest level in their field sometimes have a hard time identifying what separates a great team from a collection of individuals who can't seem to get it together. Some will say the key to winning is a strong work ethic. But haven't you known plenty of hardworking individuals who never worked together to reach their potential? Others believe that great teams are the result of chemistry. But they often say, "I can't explain how you create it, but I definitely know it when I see it." How can you get your hands around that and learn from it to build *your* team?

As a communicator who spends countless hours speaking to live audiences every year, I am always looking for straightforward ways to teach people complex truths. That's what a communicator does—he takes something complicated and makes it simple. In 1998, I wrote *The 21 Irrefutable Laws of Leadership.* My desire was to share what I had learned from three decades of leading people. The response was overwhelming. The book landed on bestseller lists of the *New York Times* Business Books, the *Wall Street Journal, Business Week,* and the Christian Booksellers Association (CBA) marketplace. For that I am truly grateful. But more important, during the last several years as I have taught the laws throughout the United States and on five continents, I have had the delight of seeing people connect with the laws, apply them to their lives, and improve their leadership. Learning the laws changed people's lives, and I knew that I had found an effective handle for helping people learn leadership.

My desire is to make team building as simple to grasp, retain, and put into practice as leadership. I want to take the mystery out of it. That's why I've worked hard to identify the Laws of Teamwork. The wonderful thing about a law is that you can depend on it. No matter who you are, what your background is, or what circumstances you face; you can take a law to the bank.

As I teach you the laws, you will find that I often approach the subject of teamwork from a leader's point of view—that makes sense since leaders are the ones who bring teams together and lead them to victory. But you don't have to be a leader to benefit from this book. Just about everything you do depends on teamwork. It doesn't matter whether you are a leader or follower, coach or player, teacher or student, parent or child, CEO or nonprofit volunteer worker. No matter who you are, if you learn and apply the laws, your teamwork capacity will increase. The greater the number of laws that you and your teammates learn, the more likely you are to be transformed from a group of individuals into a winning team.

Teams come in all shapes and sizes. If you're married, you and your spouse are a team. If you are employed by an organization, you and your colleagues are a team. If you volunteer your time, you and your fellow workers are a team. As Dan Devine joked, "A team is a team is a team. Shakespeare said that many times." Although the gifted playwright might not have said exactly that, the concept is nonetheless true. That's why teamwork is so important.

At a recent conference where I was teaching, a young leader who was just getting started in his career came up to me and asked, "John, what's the one thing I need to know about teamwork?"

"One thing?" I replied. "That's not an easy answer to come up with."

He persisted: "But just get me started. I want only the thing that's most important."

"All right, if you insist," I said. "The one thing you need to know about teamwork is that there is more than one thing you need to know about teamwork."

At first he looked at me questioningly. Then he became a bit irritated. But then I could see a sudden understanding in his eyes.

"Oh, I get it," he said. "It's a process. Okay, okay. I'm ready to dive in. I'm willing to take the time to learn."

I want to encourage you to do the same, to devote yourself to the process of learning to be a great team member and team builder. As you read about the Laws of Teamwork and begin to apply them, I think you will find that they have a positive impact on every aspect of your life. As you proceed, also remember this: None of the laws stand alone, but they all stand together really well. The greater number of laws you learn, the better you will become.

Enjoy the process, give it your best, and never forget that no matter what you want to do in life, it takes teamwork to make the dream work.

1

THE LAW OF SIGNIFICANCE

One Is Too Small a Number to Achieve Greatness

Who are your personal heroes? Okay, maybe you don't have heroes exactly. Then let me ask you this: Which people do you admire most? Who do you wish you were more like? Which people fire you up and get your juices flowing? Do you admire . . .

- Business innovators, such as Jeff Bezos, Fred Smith, or Bill Gates?
- Great athletes, such as Michael Jordan, Marion Jones, or Mark McGwire?
- Creative geniuses, such as Pablo Picasso, Buckminster Fuller, or Wolfgang Amadeus Mozart?
- Pop culture icons, such as Madonna, Andy Warhol, or Elvis Presley?

- Spiritual leaders, such as John Wesley, Billy Graham, or Mother Teresa?
- Political leaders, such as Alexander the Great, Charlemagne, or Winston Churchill?
- Film industry giants, such as D. W. Griffith, Charlie Chaplin, or Steven Spielberg?
- Architects and engineers, such as Frank Lloyd Wright, the Starrett brothers, or Joseph Strauss?
- Revolutionary thinkers, such as Marie Curie, Thomas Edison, or Albert Einstein?

Or maybe your list includes people in a field I didn't mention.

It's safe to say that we all admire achievers. And we Americans especially love pioneers and bold individualists, people who fight alone, despite the odds or opposition: the settler who carves a place for himself in the wilds of the frontier, the Old West sheriff who resolutely faces an enemy in a gunfight, the pilot who bravely flies solo across the Atlantic Ocean, and the scientist who changes the world through the power of his mind.

The Myth of the Lone Ranger

As much as we admire solo achievement, the truth is that no lone individual has done anything of value. The belief that one person can do something great is a myth. There are no real Rambos who can take on a hostile army by themselves. Even the Lone Ranger wasn't really a loner. Everywhere he went he rode with Tonto!

Nothing of significance was ever achieved by an individual acting alone. Look below the surface and you will find that all seemingly solo acts are really team efforts. Frontiersman Daniel Boone had companions from the Transylvania Company as he blazed the Wilderness Road. Sheriff Wyatt Earp had his two brothers and Doc Holliday looking out for him. Aviator Charles Lindbergh had the backing of nine businessmen from St. Louis and the services of the Ryan Aeronautical Company, which built his plane. Even Albert Einstein, the scientist who revolutionized the world with his theory of relativity, didn't work in a vacuum. Of the debt he owed to others for his work, Einstein once remarked, "Many times a day I realize how much my own outer and inner life is built upon the labors of my fellow men, both living and dead, and how earnestly I must exert myself in order to give in return as much as I have received." It's true that the history of our country is marked by the accomplishments of many strong leaders and innovative individuals who took considerable risks. But those people always were part of teams.

> *The belief that one person can do something great is a myth.*

Economist Lester C. Thurow commented on the subject:

> There is nothing antithetical in American history, culture, or traditions to teamwork. Teams were important in America's history—wagon trains conquered the West, men working together on the assembly line in American industry conquered the world, a successful national strategy and a lot of teamwork put an American on the moon first (and thus far, last). But American mythology extols only the individual . . . In America, halls of fame exist for almost every conceivable activity, but nowhere do Americans raise monuments in praise of teamwork.

I must say that I don't agree with all of Thurow's conclusions. After all, I've seen the U.S. Marine Corps war memorial in Washington, D.C., commemorating the raising of the flag on Iwo Jima. But he is right about something. Teamwork is and always has been essential to building this country. And that statement can be made about every country around the world.

The Value of Teamwork

A Chinese proverb states, "Behind an able man there are always other able men." The truth is that teamwork is at the heart of great achievement. The question isn't whether teams have value. The question is whether we acknowledge that fact and become better team players. That's why I assert that *one is too small a number to achieve greatness.* You cannot do anything of *real* value alone. That is the Law of Significance.

> *"There are no problems we cannot solve together, and very few that we can solve by ourselves."*
>
> —LYNDON JOHNSON

I challenge you to think of *one* act of genuine significance in the history of humankind that was performed by a lone human being. No matter what you name, you will find that a team of people was involved. That is why President Lyndon Johnson said, "There are no problems we cannot solve together, and very few that we can solve by ourselves."

C. Gene Wilkes, in his book *Jesus on Leadership,* observed that the power of teams not only is evident in today's modern business world, but it also has a deep history that is evident even in biblical times. Wilkes asserts,

- Teams involve more people, thus affording more resources, ideas, and energy than would an individual.
- Teams maximize a leader's potential and minimize her weaknesses. Strengths and weaknesses are more exposed in individuals.
- Teams provide multiple perspectives on how to meet a need or reach a goal, thus devising several alternatives for each situation. Individual insight is seldom as broad and deep as a group's when it takes on a problem.
- Teams share the credit for victories and the blame for losses. This fosters genuine humility and authentic community. Individuals take credit and blame alone. This fosters pride and sometimes a sense of failure.
- Teams keep leaders accountable for the goal. Individuals connected to no one can change the goal without accountability.
- Teams can simply do more than an individual.

If you want to reach your potential or strive for the seemingly impossible—such as communicating your message two thousand years after you are gone—you need to become a team player. It may be a cliché, but it is nonetheless true: Individuals play the game, but teams win championships.

Why Do We Stand Alone?

Knowing all that we do about the potential of teams, why do some people still want to do things by themselves? I believe there are a number of reasons.

1. Ego

Few people are fond of admitting that they can't do everything, yet that is a reality of life. There are no supermen or superwomen. As Kerry Walls, one of the people on my INJOY Group team, says, "Spinning more plates doesn't increase your talent—it increases your likelihood of dropping a plate." So the question is not whether you can do everything by yourself; it's how soon you're going to realize that you can't.

> *Teamwork is birthed when you concentrate on "we" instead of "me."*

Philanthropist Andrew Carnegie declared, "It marks a big step in your development when you come to realize that other people can help you do a better job than you could do alone." To do something really big, let go of your ego, and get ready to be part of a team.

2. Insecurity

In my work with leaders, I've found that some individuals fail to promote teamwork because they feel threatened by other people. Sixteenth-century Florentine statesman Niccolo Machiavelli probably made similar observations, prompting him to write, "The first method for estimating the intelligence of a ruler is to look at the men he has around him."

I believe that insecurity, rather than poor judgment or lack of intelligence, most often causes leaders to surround themselves with weak people. As I stated in *The 21 Irrefutable Laws of Leadership,* only secure leaders give power to others. That is the Law of Empowerment. On the other hand, insecure leaders usually fail to build teams because of one of two reasons: Either they want to maintain control over everything for which they are responsible, or they fear being replaced by someone more capable. In either case, leaders who fail to promote teamwork undermine their own potential and erode the best efforts of the people with whom they work. They would benefit from the advice of President Woodrow Wilson: "We should not only use all the brains we have, but all that we can borrow."

> *"We should not only use all the brains we have, but all that we can borrow."*
>
> —WOODROW WILSON

3. Naïveté

Consultant John Ghegan keeps a sign on his desk that says, "If I had it to do all over again, I'd get help." That remark accurately represents the feelings of the third type of people who fail to become team builders. They naively underestimate the difficulty of achieving big things. As a result, they try to go it alone.

Some people who start out in this group turn out okay in the end. They discover that their dreams are bigger than their capabilities, they realize they won't accomplish their goals solo, and they adjust. They make team building their approach to achievement. But some others learn the truth too late, and as a result, they never accomplish their goals. And that's a shame.

4. Temperament

Some people aren't very outgoing and simply don't think in terms of team building and team participation. As they face challenges, it never occurs to them to enlist others to achieve something.

As a people person, I find that hard to relate to. Whenever I face any kind of challenge, the very first thing I do is to think about the people I want on the team to help with it. I've been that way since I was a kid. I've

> *"People have been known to achieve more as a result of working with others than against them."*
>
> —DR. ALLAN FROMME

always thought, *Why take the journey alone when you can invite others along with you?*

I understand that not everyone operates that way. But whether or not you are naturally inclined to be part of a team is really irrelevant. If you do everything alone and never partner with other people, you create huge barriers to your own potential. Dr. Allan Fromme quipped, "People have been known to achieve more as a result of working with others than against them." What an understatement! It takes a team to do anything of lasting value. Besides, even the most introverted person in the world can learn to enjoy the benefits of being on a team. (That's true even if someone isn't trying to accomplish something great.)

A few years ago my friend Chuck Swindoll wrote a piece in *The Finishing Touch* that sums up the importance of teamwork. He said,

> Nobody is a whole team . . . We need each other. You need someone and someone needs you. Isolated islands we're not. To make this thing called life work, we gotta lean and support. And relate and respond. And give and take. And confess and forgive. And reach out and embrace and rely . . . Since none of us is a whole, independent, self-sufficient, super-capable, all-powerful hotshot, let's quit acting like we are. Life's lonely enough without our playing that silly role. The game is over. Let's link up.

For the person trying to do everything alone, the game really is over. If you want to do something big, you must link up with others. *One is too small a number to achieve greatness.* That's the Law of Significance.

YOU CAN SEE THE DIFFERENCE

When you look at the way people conduct their lives, you can tell fairly quickly who recognizes and embraces the truth of the Law of Significance. That is certainly true of Lilly Tartikoff. I don't know whether Lilly always knew the value of teamwork, but I suspect she learned it early since she was once a professional ballet dancer. If dancers don't work together, then their performances never reach the caliber of Lilly's. Beginning at age seven, she spent ten hours a day, six days a week, practicing or performing ballet. As a result she became a member of the New York City Ballet Company and performed with them from 1971 to 1980.

At a tennis party in Los Angeles in 1980, Lilly met Brandon Tartikoff, the newly named president of entertainment for NBC. At that time he was the youngest network president in history at age thirty. They soon became friends. Then they began to see each other romantically. In 1982, they were married. And that started a whole new life for Lilly. She went from a nontelevision watcher to the spouse of a network executive immersed in the L.A. culture of the entertainment industry. But that adjustment was nothing compared to the other challenge she faced that year. For the second time in his life, Brandon was diagnosed with Hodgkin's disease.

AMAZING SCIENCE

On the advice of a physician friend, Brandon went to see a young oncological researcher at UCLA named Denny Slamon. In August 1982, Dr. Slamon started Brandon on two kinds of treatment, one of which was experimental. Brandon would usually be treated on a

Friday, and afterward Lilly would drive him home and take care of him while he suffered from horrible side effects all weekend. They followed that pattern for a year, and all the while Brandon continued in his role of network president. It was a difficult time for them, but they chose to face the cancer as a team, and in time Brandon recovered.

Out of that ordeal came many things. For one, Brandon's network, NBC, went from worst to first in the ratings. In his autobiography he wrote, "Cancer helps you see things more clearly. The disease, I've found, can actually *help* you do your job, and there's a very simple reason why: There's nothing like cancer to keep you focused on what's important."[1] That focus enabled him to air some of the most popular and groundbreaking shows in television's history: *The Cosby Show, Cheers, Hill Street Blues, Miami Vice, The Golden Girls, The A-Team, St. Elsewhere,* and others.

For Lilly, though, there was a different outcome. Once Hodgkin's disease had been driven from her husband's body, she didn't simply move on.

"Brandon was at the receiving end of some pretty amazing science," she observed. The medical research that had extended Brandon's life intrigued her. So when she had an opportunity to help others benefit from that same science, she couldn't say no. That occurred in 1989 when Dr. Dennis Slamon, the UCLA scientist who had treated Brandon seven years before, asked Lilly for her help.

Nobody Can Do It Alone

For years Dr. Slamon had been studying breast cancer. He believed he was on the verge of developing a radical new treatment that would not only be more effective in treating the disease than anything previously developed, but he could do it without all the usual side effects of chemotherapy. He had the expertise and skill necessary to do the work, but he couldn't do it alone. He needed someone to help with funding. He thought of Lilly. She was only too happy to agree to assist him.

The plan she developed showed keen insight into teamwork and strategic partnerships. Lilly had once worked as a beauty adviser for Max Factor, formerly connected to Revlon. She sought to get Ronald Perelman, the CEO of Revlon, together with Dr. Slamon. At first that wasn't easy, but once Perelman realized the potential of Slamon's research, he pledged $2.4 million to the scientist's work with no restrictions. It was a partnership unlike anything that had been done before. What resulted was the creation of the Revlon/UCLA Women's Cancer Research Program—and a successful new treatment for cancer was soon saving women's lives.

A Taste of Teamwork

For Lilly, cofounding the research program was just a beginning. She had gotten a taste of what teamwork could do, and she was hungry to do much more. She quickly realized that she could enlist others to her cause. She would build a larger team, and she would use her show business connections to do it. That same year she established an annual Fire and Ice Ball in Hollywood to raise money. A few years later, she enlarged her circle and partnered with the Entertainment Industry Foundation (EIF) and created the Revlon Run/Walk, first in Los Angeles, and then in New York. So far, those events have raised more than $18 million for cancer research. And in 1996, she helped create the National Women's Cancer Research Alliance.

In 1997, her husband Brandon's cancer recurred a third time, and it took his life. He was only forty-eight years old. Despite the personal setback, Lilly continues to build teams to fight cancer. When she met Katie Couric, who had lost her husband to colon cancer, Lilly was again inspired to action. With the help of Couric and the EIF, she formed the National Colorectal Cancer Research Alliance in 2000.

"When I sat down with Katie," said Lilly, "to hear that, with an early diagnosis, you could turn the cancer around, and literally, it's 90 percent curable and preventable. Well, this was like putting a steak in front of a hungry dog . . . I thought, we've got to do this. So I brought in all my partners: the Entertainment Industry Foundation and Dr. Slamon . . . and Dr. Slamon brought together an agenda and a mission . . . So we created the NCCRA [National Colorectal Cancer Research Alliance]. You have no idea how exciting and gratifying it is."[2]

An individual cannot do the incredible, significant task that Lilly Tartikoff and her partners are trying to accomplish. No single person can take on cancer. But that's true of anything worth doing. If it's significant, it takes a team. That's something Lilly realized, put into practice, and now lives by every day. *One is too small a number to achieve greatness.* That is the Law of Significance.

TEAMWORK THOUGHT

You may be good—but you're not *that* good!

Becoming a Better Team Member

What major goals are you working toward achieving right now? Write some of them here:

1. ______________________________

2. ______________________________

3. ______________________________

Now, reflect on how you are working toward these goals. What approach have you been taking to achieve them? Are you going it alone? Or are you building a team to accomplish them?

If you're not trying to be part of a team, figure out why. Is it a matter of ego? Are you insecure? Have you misjudged the size of the challenges? Or does your temperament incline you to work alone? If you answer yes to one of these questions, work to overcome the difficulty immediately. The sooner you become a team player, the sooner you will be able to achieve your dreams.

Becoming a Better Team Leader

Think about the greatest dream you have for your life. Now ask yourself,

- "Is it bigger than I am?"
- "Does it benefit others as well as myself?"
- "Is it worth dedicating part of my life to?"

If you answer yes to all of these questions, then think about what kinds of people should join you to achieve that dream. Make a list of the like-minded people you know who might want to join you in the process. Then invite them to take the journey with you. And be on the lookout for others who would benefit from being part of the team.

COMPANION
ONLINE
RESOURCE

Learn more about how the Law of Significance uniquely applies to you.

Take the FREE Law of Significance assessment at **LawsOfTeamwork.com**.

2

THE LAW OF THE BIG PICTURE

The Goal Is More Important Than the Role

Years ago, I was invited to participate in an important conference that was being planned by a highly respected national organization. I was one of about a dozen speakers who had been selected to speak to an audience of more than sixty thousand people drawn from all parts of the country. It was for a worthy cause that I valued, and I considered the invitation to be an honor.

Several weeks before the conference was to occur, all the speakers were scheduled to meet together along with the founder of the organization to talk strategy, discuss the topics about which we would speak, and give one another support and suggestions. I was really excited about it because the group included some extraordinary leaders. It promised to be an electric time, but the reality of the meeting turned out to be different from what I expected.

When we all got into a room together, it didn't feel like a strategy-and-support session. As we discussed the upcoming day, a few of the speakers seemed to be jockeying for position. Because they were good communicators, they understood that the speaking order, the time of day, and the amount of time allotted would make a big difference in how their messages would be received. The role each speaker was to play seemed to be of more interest than the goal of the conference.

But I also noticed something else. When one speaker briefly informed us about his topic, I sensed immediately that his speech would be the real hinge pin of the whole conference. All of the other messages would be subordinate to it. Yet the man was not fighting for the best place. He wasn't jockeying. He didn't seem to want any part of that kind of maneuvering.

In that moment when everyone was focusing on himself, I realized that we had lost sight of the big picture of why we were there. So I said to the group about this speaker, "I believe his message will be the difference maker in the lives of the people attending this conference. And I think the audience will receive it better if it's delivered when I am slated to speak. Please," I said to the person who wasn't trying to promote himself, "take my spot."

It was almost as if somebody had struck each person in the room. Suddenly everybody regained perspective. After that, instead of looking out for themselves and protecting turf, all of the speakers were willing to give everything for the common good. We all remembered that the goal was more important than our individual roles. That is the essence of the Law of the Big Picture.

What's in It for Me?

In a culture that sings the praises of individual gold medals and where a person fights for rights instead of focusing on taking responsibility, people tend to lose sight of the big picture. In fact, some people seem to believe that they *are* the entire picture: Everything revolves around their needs, their goals, and their desires. I saw a message on a T-shirt that expresses the attitude well: "My idea of a team is a whole lot of people doing what I tell them to do."

> *If you think you are the entire picture, you will never see the big picture.*

A team isn't supposed to be a bunch of people being used as a tool by one individual for selfish gain. Members of a team must have mutually beneficial shared goals. They must be motivated to work together, not manipulated by someone for individual glory. Anyone who is accustomed to pulling together people and using them to benefit only himself isn't a team builder; he's a dictator.

If you want to observe team dynamics in action, look at the world of sports where you can easily see whether people are working together. The outcome of a game is immediate and measurable. For that reason it's easy to see when an individual is thinking only of himself and not the shared goals and values of the team.

To win in sports, members of the team must always keep the big picture in front of them. They must remember that the goal is more important than their role—or any individual glory they may desire. NBA superstar David Robinson remarked, "I think any player will tell you that individual accomplishments help your ego, but if you don't win, it makes for a very, very long season. It counts more that the team has played well."

It's All About the Team

The acclaimed football coach of Oklahoma during the 1950s, Bud Wilkinson, put it this way in *The Book of Football Wisdom:* "If a team is to reach its potential, each player must be willing to subordinate his personal goals to the good of the team."

> *"If a team is to reach its potential, each player must be willing to subordinate his personal goals to the good of the team."*
>
> —BUD WILKINSON

Some sports teams seem to embrace an "everyone-for-himself" mind-set. Others weave the attitude of subordination and teamwork into the fabric of everything they do. For example, football teams such as Notre Dame and Penn State don't put the names of the players on their jerseys. Lou Holtz, former coach of the Fighting Irish, once explained why. He said, "At Notre Dame, we believed the interlocking ND was all the identification you needed. Whenever anyone complained, I told them they were lucky we allowed numbers on the uniforms. Given my druthers, I would have nothing more than initials indicating what position the wearer played. If your priority is the team rather than yourself, what else do you need?"

Winning teams have players who put the good of the team ahead of themselves. They want to play in their area of strength, but they're willing to do what it takes to take care of the team. They are willing to sacrifice their role for the greater goal. That's the Law of the Big Picture.

Seeing the Big Picture

People who build successful teams never forget that every person on a team has a role to play, and every role plays its part in contributing to the bigger picture. Without that perspective the team cannot accomplish its goal, whether the team's "game" is sports, business, family, ministry, or government.

Leaders at the highest level understand the Law of the Big Picture. They continually keep the vision of the big picture before themselves and their people. An outstanding example involves Winston Churchill. It's said that during World War II when Britain was experiencing its darkest days, the country had a difficult time keeping men working in the coal mines. Many wanted to give up their dirty, thankless jobs in the dangerous mines to join military service, which garnered much public praise and support. Yet their work in the mines was critical to the success of the war. Without coal the military and the people at home would be in trouble.

So the prime minister faced thousands of coal miners one day and told them of their importance to the war effort, how their role could make or break the goal of maintaining England's freedom.

Churchill painted a picture of what it would be like when the war ended, of the grand parade that would honor the people who fought the war. First would come the sailors of the navy, he said, the people who continued the tradition of Trafalgar and the defeat of the Spanish Armada. Next would come the best and brightest of Britain, the pilots of the Royal Air Force who fended off the German Luftwaffe. Following them would be the soldiers who had fought at Dunkirk.

Then last of all would come the coal-dust-covered men in miners' caps. And Churchill indicated that someone from the crowd might say, "And where were you during the critical days of the struggle?"

And the voices of ten thousand men would respond, "We were deep in the earth with our faces to the coal."

It's said that tears appeared in the eyes of those hardened men. And they returned to their inglorious work with steely resolve, having been reminded of the role they were playing in their country's noble goal of preserving freedom for the Western world.

> *"Everybody on a championship team doesn't get publicity, but everyone can say he's a champion."*
>
> —EARVIN "MAGIC" JOHNSON

That's the kind of mind-set it takes to build a team. It takes the courage and the resolve to recognize that *the goal is more important than the role.* It's no small thing for people to do what's best for the team. Often it means sacrificing professional satisfaction, individual statistics, or personal glory. But as NBA star-turned-successful-businessman Earvin "Magic" Johnson says, "Everybody on a championship team doesn't get publicity, but everyone can say he's a champion."

What's Up with Big Picture Teams?

So how do people start to become a more unified team? How do individuals make the shift from independent people to team players who exemplify the Law of the Big Picture? It's not something that happens overnight. It takes time. Here is my best take on how to get the process started.

1. Look Up *at the Big Picture*

Everything starts with vision. You need to have a goal. Without one you cannot have a real team. Hall of Fame catcher Yogi Berra joked, "If you don't know where you're going, you'll end up somewhere else." An individual without a goal may end up anywhere. A group of individuals without a goal can go nowhere. On the other hand, if everyone in a group embraces the vision for achieving the big picture, then the people have the potential to become an effective team.

Leaders usually have the role of capturing and communicating vision. They must see it first and then help everyone else to see it. That was what Winston Churchill did when he spoke to the coal miners during the war. That was what Dr. Martin Luther King Jr. did as he spoke to people about his dream from the steps of the Lincoln Monument in Washington, D.C. That was what GE CEO Jack Welch did when he let his people know that a division of GE that couldn't be first or second in its market wouldn't be a part of GE. The people on a team will sacrifice and work together *only* if they can see what they're working toward.

If you are the leader of your team, your role is to do what only you can do: Paint the big picture for your people. Without the vision they will not find the desire to achieve the goal.

2. **Size Up** *the Situation*

One value of seeing the big picture is that it helps you recognize how far you really are from achieving it. For someone determined to do everything alone, seeing the gulf between what is and what could be is often intimidating. But for people who live to build teams, seeing the size of the task ahead doesn't worry them. They don't shrink from the challenge—they savor the opportunity. They can't wait to put together a team and a plan to accomplish that vision.

At a meeting of all three divisions of The INJOY Group, CEO Dave Sutherland stood before our people and outlined a few of our goals for the coming year. (Some of those goals were huge.) During that process, Dave said, "Some people see the size of the goal, and they get scared. That doesn't bother me a bit. We've already got a great team. To make it to the next level, we just need a few more people like the ones we already have." That's the mind-set of a team builder!

3. Line Up *Needed Resources*

Hawley R. Everhart believes, "It's all right to aim high if you have plenty of ammunition." That's what resources are: ammunition to help you reach a goal. It doesn't matter what kind of team you're on. You cannot make progress without the support of the appropriate equipment, facilities, funds, and so forth—whether your goal is climbing a mountain, capturing a market, or creating a ministry. The better resourced the team is, the fewer distractions the players will have as they try to achieve their goal.

4. Call Up *the Right Players*

When it comes to building a successful team, the players are everything. You can have a distinct vision, a precise plan, plenty of resources, and incredible leadership, but if you don't have the right people, you're not going to get anywhere. (I'll talk more about this in several of the other laws.) You can lose with good players, but you cannot win with bad ones.

5. Give Up *Personal Agendas*

Teams that win have players who continually ask themselves, "What's best for the rest?" They continually set aside their personal agendas for the good of the team. Their motto can be expressed by the words of Ray Kroc, founder of McDonald's, who said, "No one of us is more important than the rest of us."

A remarkable sports story from several years ago was the success of the U.S. Women's Soccer Team. They won the Olympic gold medal and the World Cup in a few brief years. A key player on that team was Mia Hamm. In her book *Go for the Goal,* she gives her perspective on her sport and the attitude a player must bring into the game to achieve the goal of becoming a champion:

> *"No one of us is more important than the rest of us."*
>
> —RAY KROC

> Soccer is not an individual sport. I don't score all the goals, and the ones I do score are usually the product of a team effort. I don't keep the ball out of the back of the net on the other end of the field. I don't plan our game tactics. I don't wash our training gear (okay, sometimes I do), and I don't make our airline reservations. I am a member of a team, and I rely on the team. I defer to it and sacrifice for it, because the team, not the individual, is the ultimate champion.

Mia Hamm understands the Law of the Big Picture. And by doing whatever it took to help her team—including washing the gear—she demonstrated that the goal was more important than the role.

6. Step Up *to a Higher Level*

Only when players come together and give up their own agendas can a team move up to a higher level. That's the kind of sacrifice required for teamwork. Unfortunately some people prefer to cling to agendas and pursue the paths of their own inflated egos instead of letting go of them to achieve something greater than themselves.

It's just as philosopher Friedrich Nietzsche said: "Many are stubborn in pursuit of the path they have chosen, few in pursuit of the goal." And that's a shame because people who think only of themselves are missing the big picture. As a result their potential goes untapped, and the people who are depending on them are bound to be let down.

Subordinate Role for the Team's Success

President Abraham Lincoln once remarked, "Nearly all men can stand adversity, but if you want to test a man's character, give him power." Few people have more power than an American president. Being the so-called leader of the free world can certainly go to a person's head. But not to Jimmy Carter's. If you review his career—from the time he was a school board official to his term in the White House and beyond—you can see that he was willing to take on nearly any role to achieve a goal he believed in. He has always embraced the importance of the big picture.

There is possibly no more vivid example of the Law of the Big Picture in Carter's life than his work with Habitat for Humanity. Habitat was officially founded by Millard and Linda Fuller in 1976, though the two had been exploring the idea for many years before that, first in the U.S. and then overseas. The goal of the organization is a huge one—to eliminate poverty-level housing and homelessness from the world.

In the late seventies and early eighties, they began their bold venture. After six years they had built houses internationally in Mexico, Zaire, and Guatemala. And in the U.S., they had affiliates building houses in San Antonio, Texas; Americus, Georgia; Johns Island, South Carolina; and other locations in Florida and Appalachia. Groundwork was being laid for them to build in many other cities, but the process was a struggle. They had found a successful formula for their goal: Offer home ownership to the neediest people able to make a house payment, build low-cost housing using volunteer labor, involve the future home owner in the building process, and create no-interest loans to finance the houses. It was an inspired idea, and it was catching on. To reach the world as they desired, however, the Fullers knew they would have to take Habitat to a whole new level.

From their headquarters in the town of Americus in southern Georgia, the Fullers saw a possibility. Ten miles away in the tiny town of Plains was a man who might be able to help them: Jimmy Carter. The former U.S. president had spoken at a couple of Habitat functions. Following Carter's speaking in 1983, Millard Fuller got the idea to approach Carter about helping the project along. And in early 1984 they made contact. When Carter said he was very interested in Habitat for Humanity, Fuller decided to boldly propose a list of fifteen possible roles the former president could take, hoping he would agree to one or two. His list included serving on Habitat's board, making media contacts, helping to raise money, doing a thirty-minute video, and working on a building crew for a day.

To Fuller's surprise, Carter did not agree to do one or two items on the list. He agreed to do *everything* on it. Ironically the task that captured the attention of the public most was Carter's willingness to serve on a building crew and swing a hammer to help construct a house. At first people thought Carter would just stop by for brief publicity photos. But the former president put together a work crew, traveled with them via Trailways bus to the Brooklyn, New York, building site, worked tenaciously every day for a week, and slept in a church basement along with everyone else. That first time was in 1984. Carter has raised a team and served in similar fashion every year since then. And his dedicated service has attracted people from every walk of life to serve in similar roles.[1]

A Shared Goal

Habitat for Humanity is the brainchild of the Fullers, and its success is the result of the efforts of hundreds of thousands of people from around the globe. But Jimmy Carter is the one who put it on the map. His selfless service inspired people rich and poor, famous and obscure, powerful and not so powerful to see the huge goal of helping people at the lowest level of society by providing them with a decent place to live. And he inspired them to get involved.

So far Habitat and its volunteers have built more than 100,000 houses sheltering more than a half million people all over the world.[2] Why? Because they, like Carter, wanted to be part of something bigger than themselves. They understood that the goal was more important than the role. They embraced the truth of the Law of the Big Picture.

Teamwork Thought

When you see the big picture correctly,
you serve the team more quickly.

Becoming a Better Team Member

What goal in your life is bigger than you are? Are you currently participating in something greater than yourself? If not, set aside some time to spend alone reflecting on your goals and priorities. If you are trying to accomplish something big, then ask yourself what you are willing to do to accomplish it. Are you willing to take a subordinate role if necessary for the good of the team, as President Carter did? If not, you may become a hindrance to the success of the team.

Becoming a Better Team Leader

Think about a team you are currently part of (preferably one with a big goal). What kind of attitude do team members have when it comes to the big picture? Are they team players who desire to do whatever it takes for the team to succeed? Or do they desire to benefit only themselves?

Begin to foster a team mind-set in others by modeling a willingness to serve the big picture rather than yourself. Then think about ways you can help your teammates to embrace the Law of the Big Picture. Motivate people by painting the big picture. Publicly honor team play. And give rewards to people who sacrifice for the good of the team.

COMPANION ONLINE RESOURCE

Learn more about how the Law of the Big Picture uniquely applies to you.

Take the FREE Law of the Big Picture assessment at **LawsOfTeamwork.com**.

3

THE LAW OF THE NICHE

All Players Have a Place Where They Add the Most Value

On January 26, 2001, the United States experienced a historic first: An African-American assumed the post of secretary of state, the highest cabinet post in the United States government. The man who took that position was Colin Powell. Columnist Carl Rowan remarked of the appointment, "To understand the significance of Powell's elevation to this extremely difficult and demanding post, you must realize that only a generation ago it was an unwritten rule that in the foreign affairs field, blacks could serve only as ambassador to Liberia and minister to the Canary Islands."

Powell's appointment was remarkable, but not just because it was groundbreaking. It was significant because, to put it simply, Colin Powell was the best individual in all of the United States to take on the role of secretary of state. George W. Bush, the president who appointed him, stated, "In this cause, I know of no better person to be the face and voice of American diplomacy than Colin Powell," citing his "directness of speech, his towering integrity, his deep respect for our democracy, and his soldier's sense of duty."[1] Bush recognizes that *all players have a place where they add the most value.* Powell's is running the State Department. That's the Law of the Niche.

A Place for Him

A soldier's sense of duty has been a vital part of the character of Colin Powell since he was in his early twenties. Something of a late bloomer, Powell entered college uncertain of what he wanted to do with his life. But it didn't take him long to find his identity: in an ROTC unit called the Pershing Rifles at the City College of New York. It was there that he discovered real teamwork for the first time in his life. In *My American Journey,* Powell wrote:

> My experience in high school, on basketball and track teams, and briefly in Boy Scouting had never produced a sense of belonging or many permanent friendships. The Pershing Rifles did. For the first time in my life I was a member of a brotherhood . . . The discipline, the structure, the camaraderie, the sense of belonging were what I craved. I became a leader almost immediately. I found a selflessness among the ranks that reminded me of the caring atmosphere within my family. Race, color, background, income meant nothing. The PRs [Pershing Rifles] would go the limit for each other and for the group. If this was what soldiering was all about, then maybe I wanted to be a soldier.[2]

As he got closer to graduation from college, there was no doubt in his mind. He gladly chose military life.

No Ordinary Journey

In the army Powell seemed to achieve success everywhere he went and quickly rose in rank. His love was commanding troops, and when he received those assignments, he did well. Yet he was constantly tapped for special jobs and responsibilities. When that happened again and again, keeping him from leading soldiers in the field, he became frustrated. But a mentor, General John Wickham, wisely told him, "You're not going to have a conventional army career. Some officers are just not destined for it."

Wickham was right. Powell's career did turn out to be unusual. And it ultimately prepared him for a cabinet post, sharpening his gifts and giving him broad experience. As an infantry officer who did tours around the globe (including two in Vietnam), Powell learned command and leadership. His work with soldiers also taught him to communicate and connect with people. As a White House Fellow, he got his first exposure to American politics and world governments. Besides his interaction with high-level U.S. officials, he met with leaders of Japan, the Soviet Union, China, Poland, Bulgaria, and West Germany.

Powell moved to a whole new level in his post at the Pentagon during the Carter and Reagan administrations. It was there that he learned how to work with civil servants and he expanded his understanding of government and military politics. As the senior military assistant to Secretary of Defense Caspar Weinberger, Powell traveled the world and attained in-depth comprehension of the complex relationships between the United States and foreign powers.

But in the office of the national security adviser, Powell stepped into the big leagues. As the deputy assistant to the president for national security affairs, he gained valuable experience in foreign policy. In fact, he was so adept that when his boss, Frank Carlucci, was asked to be secretary of defense, Powell stepped into Carlucci's former position as national security adviser. There he not only advised President Reagan, but Powell worked side by side with Secretary of State George Shultz as the statesman negotiated nuclear missile treaties with the USSR, organized summits between heads of state, and worked with Soviet President Mikhail Gorbachev to end the cold war.

Command Performance

How does someone like Colin Powell top off a successful term as the nation's first African-American national security adviser? By achieving the military's highest rank of four stars, and then by becoming the youngest chairman of the Joint Chiefs of Staff in the history of the nation. (He was also that position's first African-American and first ROTC graduate.) And once again, Powell shone in his position. Les Aspin, former secretary of defense, commented about Powell following a meeting in the Clinton White House, "It was so clear to all of us that he could do any job in the room, up to and including president."[3]

When President-elect Bush approached him about becoming a cabinet member, there was only one logical place for him to serve, the place where he would add the most. At a town hall meeting on January 25, 2001, Powell remarked,

> I didn't know I would be coming back into government when I left the Army seven years ago and went into private life . . . But when Governor Bush asked me to consider it, I was ready for it. I was anxious to see if I could serve again. I think I have something to contribute still. And when he specifically said, I would like you to go to the State Department, it was almost as if I had been preparing for this in one way or another for many, many years. My work in the Pentagon, my work as a Deputy National Security Adviser, National Security Adviser, Chairman of the Joint Chiefs of Staff, and seven years in private life watching the world change, suggested to me this is something I should do.[4]

President Bush, his cabinet, and everyone in the country have a lot to gain from Powell. Not only is he the best person for the job, but he has given the newly elected president and his team greater credibility with a constituency inclined not to trust them. Powell's appointment is tangible proof of Bush's claim to inclusiveness. But that's the power of the Law of the Niche. When the right team member is in the right place, everyone benefits.

Good things happen to a team when a player takes the place where he adds the most value. Great things happen when all the players on the team take the role that maximizes their strengths—their talent, skill, and experience. That's the power of the Law of the Niche.

When People Are in the Wrong Place

Just about everyone has experienced being on some kind of team where people had to take on roles that didn't suit them: an accountant forced to work with people all day, a basketball forward forced to play center, a guitarist filling in on keyboard, a teacher stuck doing paperwork, a spouse who hates the kitchen taking on the role of cook.

What happens to a team when one or more of its members constantly play out of position? First, morale erodes because the team isn't playing up to its capability. Then people become resentful. The people working in an area of weakness resent that their best is untapped. And other people on the team who know that they could better fill a mismatched position on the team resent that their skills are being overlooked. Before long, people become unwilling to work as a team. Then everyone's confidence begins to erode. And the situation just keeps getting worse. The team stops progressing, and the competition takes advantage of the team's obvious weaknesses. As a result the team never realizes its potential. When people aren't where they do things well, things don't turn out well. That's the Law of the Niche.

Having the right people in the right places is essential to team building. A team's dynamic changes according to the placement of people:

The Wrong Person in the Wrong Place	=	Regression
The Wrong Person in the Right Place	=	Frustration
The Right Person in the Wrong Place	=	Confusion
The Right Person in the Right Place	=	Progression
The Right People in the Right Places	=	Multiplication

It doesn't matter what kind of team you're dealing with, the principles are the same. David Ogilvy was right when he said, "A well-run restaurant is like a winning baseball team. It makes the most of every crew member's talent and takes advantage of every split-second opportunity to speed up service."

I was reminded of the Law of the Niche by something I did a few years ago. I had been asked to write a chapter for a book called *Destiny and Deliverance,* which was tied to the DreamWorks movie *The Prince of Egypt.* It was a wonderful, delightful experience. During the writing process, I was invited to go to California and view parts of the movie while it was still in production. That made me want to do something I had never done before: attend a movie premiere in Hollywood.

My publisher managed to get me a pair of tickets for the premiere, and when the time arrived, my wife, Margaret, and I flew out to the movie capital. Movie stars and moviemakers, along with many other people in the industry, attended the high-energy event. Margaret and I enjoyed the movie—and the whole experience—immensely. In short, we had a blast.

Now, anybody who's gone to a movie, show, or sporting event with me knows my pattern. As soon as I am pretty certain about the outcome of a ball game, I hit the exit to beat the crowds. When the Broadway audience is giving the ovation, I'm gone. And the second the credits begin to roll in a movie, I'm out of my seat. As *The Prince of Egypt* came to a close, I started to get up, but not a person in the theater moved. And then something really surprising happened. As the credits rolled, people began to applaud the lesser-known individuals whose names appeared on the screen: the costume designer, the gaffer, the key grip, the assistant director. It was a moment I'll never forget—and a distinct reminder of the Law of the Niche: *All players have a place where they add the most value.* When each person does the job that's best for him, everybody wins.

Put People in Their Place

NFL champion coach Vince Lombardi observed, "The achievements of an organization are the results of the combined effort of each individual." That is true, but creating a winning team doesn't come just from having the right individuals. You may have a group of talented individuals, but if each person is not doing what adds the most value to the team, you won't achieve your potential as a team. That's the art of leading a team. You've got to put people in their places—and I mean that in the most positive way!

To be able to put people in the places that utilize their talents and maximize the team's potential, you need three things:

You Must Know the Team

You cannot build a winning team or organization if you don't know its vision, purpose, culture, or history. If you don't know where the team is trying to go—and why it's trying to get there—you cannot take the team to the height of its potential. You've got to start where the team actually is; only then can you take it somewhere.

You Must Know the Situation

Even though the vision or purpose of an organization may be fairly constant, its situation changes constantly. Good team builders know where the team is and what the situation requires. For example, when a team is young and just getting started, the greatest priority is often to gather good people. But as a team matures and the level of talent increases, fine-tuning becomes more important. At that time a leader must spend more time matching the person to the position.

You Must Know the Player

It sounds obvious, but you must know the person you are trying to position in the right niche. I mention it because leaders tend to want to make everyone else conform to their image, to approach their work using the same skills and problem-solving methods. But team building is not working on an assembly line.

As you work to build a team, evaluate each person's experience, skills, temperament, attitude, passion, people skills, discipline, emotional strength, and potential. Only then will you be ready to help a team member find his proper place.

START BY FINDING THE RIGHT PLACE FOR YOU

Right now you may not be in a position to place others on your team. In fact, you may be thinking, *How do I find my niche?* If that's the case, then follow these guidelines:

- *Be secure.* My friend Wayne Schmidt says, "No amount of personal competency compensates for personal insecurity." If you allow your insecurities to get the better of you, you'll be inflexible and reluctant to change. And to grow, you must be willing to change.
- *Get to know yourself.* You won't be able to find your niche if you don't know your strengths and weaknesses. Spend time reflecting on and exploring your gifts. Ask others to give you feedback. Do what it takes to remove personal blind spots.
- *Trust your leader.* A good leader will help you start moving in the right direction. If you don't trust your leader, look to another mentor for help. Or get on another team.
- *See the big picture.* Your place on the team makes sense only in the context of the big picture. If your only motivation for finding your niche is personal gain, your poor motives may prevent you from discovering what you desire.

• *Rely on your experience.* When it comes down to it, the only way to know that you've discovered your niche is to try what seems right and learn from your failures and successes. When you discover what you were made for, your heart sings. It says, *There's no place like this place anywhere near this place, so this must be the place!*

> *When you discover your place, you will say, "There's no place like this place anywhere near this place, so this must be the place!"*

A Place for Everyone and Everyone in His Place

One organization that strives to match its people to the right places is the U.S. military. That is particularly true now that it employs an all-volunteer force. If each function in a military command doesn't work at top efficiency (and interact well with all the other parts), then terrible—and sometimes deadly—breakdowns occur.

Nobody is more keenly aware of that than a combat pilot. Take, for example, Charlie Plumb, who retired as a captain of the U.S. Navy. A graduate of Annapolis, he served in Vietnam in the mid-1960s, flying seventy-five missions from the aircraft carrier USS *Kitty Hawk.*

An aircraft carrier is a place where you can readily observe how all the pieces of the military puzzle come together to support each other. A carrier is often described as being like a floating city with its crew of 5,500 people, a population greater than that of some towns in which its crew members grew up. It must be self-sustaining, and each of its seventeen departments must function as a team accomplishing its mission.

Every pilot knows of the team effort required to put a jet in the air. It takes hundreds of people utilizing dozens of technical specialties to launch, monitor, support, land, and maintain an aircraft. Even more people are involved if that plane is armed for combat. Charlie Plumb undoubtedly recognized that many people worked tirelessly to keep him flying. But despite the efforts of the best-trained air support group in the world, Plumb found himself in a North Vietnamese prison as a POW after his F-4 Phantom jet was shot down on May 19, 1967, during his seventy-fifth mission.

Plumb was held prisoner for nearly six grueling years, part of the time in the infamous Hanoi Hilton. During those years, he and his fellow prisoners were humiliated, starved, tortured, and forced to live in squalid conditions. Yet he didn't let the experience break him. He now says, "Our unity through our faith in God and in our love for country were the great strength which kept us going through some very difficult times."

Turning Point

Plumb was released from his imprisonment on February 18, 1973, and continued his career in the navy. But an incident years after his return to the United States marked his life as surely as his imprisonment. One day he and his wife, Cathy, were eating in a restaurant when a man came to the table and said, "You're Plumb. You flew jet fighters in Vietnam."

"That's right," answered Plumb. "I did."

"It was fighter squadron 114 on the *Kitty Hawk*. You were shot down. You parachuted into enemy hands," the man continued. "You spent six years as a prisoner of war."

The former pilot was taken aback. He looked at the man, trying to identify him, but couldn't. "How in the world did you know that?" Plumb finally asked.

"I packed your parachute."

Plumb was staggered. All he could do was struggle to his feet and shake the man's hand. "I must tell you," Plumb finally said, "I've said a lot of prayers of thanks for your nimble fingers, but I didn't realize I'd have the opportunity of saying thanks in person."[5]

What if the navy had put the wrong person in the position of parachute rigger, the anonymous and the rarely thanked job that man performed during the Vietnam War? Charlie Plumb wouldn't have known about it until it was too late. And we wouldn't even know where the breakdown had occurred because Plumb wouldn't have lived to tell the tale.

Today, Charlie Plumb is a motivational speaker to Fortune 500 companies, government agencies, and other organizations. He often tells the story of the man who packed his parachute, and he uses it to deliver a message on teamwork. He says, "In a world where downsizing forces us to do more with less, we must empower the team. 'Packing others' parachutes' can mean the difference in survival. Yours and your team's!"[6]

That's just another way of communicating the Law of the Niche. Are you packing parachutes for your teammates? Or are you functioning at less than 100 percent? *All players have a place where they add the most value.* I want to encourage you to make sure you've found yours.

Teamwork Thought

You are most valuable where you add the most value.

Becoming a Better Team Member

Have you found your niche? As you fulfill your responsibilities, do you find yourself thinking something like, *There's no place like this place anywhere near this place, so this must be the place*? If so, then stay the course and keep growing and learning in your area of expertise. If not, you need to get on track.

If you know what your niche is but aren't working in it, start planning a transition. It could be as simple as a change in duties or as complex as a change of career. No matter whether it will require six weeks or six years, you need a transition plan and a timetable for completing it. Once you're certain of your course, have the courage to take the first step.

If you have no idea what you should be doing, you need to do some research. Talk to your spouse and close friends about your strengths and weaknesses. Ask for your leader's assessment. Take personality or temperament tests. Look for recurring themes in your life. Try to articulate your life purpose. Do whatever it takes to find clues concerning where you should be. Then try new things related to your discoveries. The only way to find your niche is to gain experience.

Becoming a Better Team Leader

A sign of a great team leader is the proper placement of people. Use the guidelines in the chapter—know your team, the situation, and the players—to begin improving your placement process. And remember this: To help people reach their potential and maximize their effectiveness, stretch them out of their comfort zones, but never out of their gift zones. Moving people outside their gifts leads to frustration, but motivating people out of their comfort zones leads to fulfillment.

A sign of a great team leader is the proper placement of people.

COMPANION ONLINE RESOURCE

Learn more about how the Law of the Niche uniquely applies to you.

Take the FREE Law of the Niche assessment at **LawsOfTeamwork.com**.

4

THE LAW OF MOUNT EVEREST

As the Challenge Escalates, the Need for Teamwork Elevates

In 1935, twenty-one-year-old Tenzing Norgay made his first trip to Mount Everest. He worked as a porter for a British team of mountaineers. A Sherpa born in the high altitudes of Nepal, Tenzing had been drawn to the mountain from the time that Westerners began visiting the area with the idea of climbing to the mountain's peak. The first group had come in 1920. Fifteen years later, climbers were still trying to figure out how to conquer the mountain.

The farthest this expedition would go was up to the North Col, which was at an altitude of 22,000 feet. (A col is a flat area along a mountain's ridge between peaks.) And it was just below that col that the climbing party made a gruesome discovery. They came across a wind-shredded tent. And in that tent was a skeleton with a little frozen skin stretched over the bones. It was sitting in an odd position, with one boot off and the laces of the other boot between its bony fingers.

Harshest Place on the Planet

Mountain climbing is not for the faint of heart because the world's highest peaks are some of the most inhospitable places on earth. Of course, that hasn't stopped people from attempting to conquer mountains. In 1786, the first climbers made it to the summit of Europe's highest mountain, Mont Blanc in France. That was quite a feat. But there's a big difference between climbing the highest of the Alps at 15,771 feet and climbing Everest, the world's highest peak at 29,035 feet, especially in the days before high-tech equipment. Everest is remote, the altitude incapacitates all but the hardiest and most experienced climbers, and the weather is ruthlessly unforgiving. Experts believe that the bodies of 120 failed climbers remain on the mountain today.[1]

The body Tenzing and the others found in 1935 was that of Maurice Wilson, an Englishman who had sneaked into Tibet and tried to climb the mountain secretly, without the permission of the Tibetan government. Because he was trying to make the ascent quietly, he had hired only three porters to climb the mountain with him. As they approached the North Col, those men had refused to go any farther with him. Wilson decided to try to make the climb on his own. That decision killed him.

Measure the Cost

Only someone who has climbed a formidable mountain knows what it takes to make it to the top. For thirty-two years, between 1920 and 1952, seven major expeditions tried—and failed—to make it to the top of Everest. Tenzing Norgay was on six of those expeditions, as well as many other high climbs to other mountains. His fellow climbers joked that he had a third lung because of his ability to climb tirelessly while carrying heavy loads. He became respected, and he learned a lot. The greatest lesson was that no one should underestimate the difficulty of the climb. He had seen people do it at the ultimate cost to themselves.

On one climb, for example, when conditions became difficult, Tenzing and the other Sherpas put on their crampons (spikes that attach to climbing boots). But George Frey, an experienced mountaineer, decided not to wear his because he thought he didn't need them. He slipped and fell one thousand feet to his death below. Tenzing regretted the man's death, but his view was realistic. He wrote of careless climbers, "Like so many men before them—they had held a great mountain too lightly, and they had paid the price."[2]

Not a Casual Stroll

In 1953, Tenzing embarked on his seventh expedition to Everest with a British group led by Colonel John Hunt. By then, he was respected not only as a porter who could carry heavy loads at high altitudes, but also as a mountaineer and full-fledged expedition member, an honor unusual at that time for a Sherpa. The year before he had climbed to a height of 28,250 feet with a Swiss team. Up to then, that was the closest any human being had come to the top of the mountain.

Tenzing was also engaged to be the British group's sirdar for the trip, the Sherpa leader who would hire, organize, and lead the porters for the journey. That was no small task. To hope to get just two people from base camp up to the summit, the team brought ten high-altitude climbers, including a New Zealander named Edmund Hillary. Altogether, the men would require two and a half *tons* of equipment and food. Those supplies couldn't be trucked or air-lifted to the base of the mountain. They had to be delivered to Kathmandu and *carried* on the backs of men and women 180 miles up and down Himalayan ridges and over rivers crossed by narrow rope-and-plank bridges to the base camp. Tenzing would have to hire between two and three hundred people just to get the supplies in the vicinity of the mountain.

Supplies needed by the party above the base camp would have to be carried up the mountain by another forty porters, each a Sherpa with extensive mountain experience. The best third of that team would continue working higher up the mountain, carrying up the 750 pounds of necessary equipment in 30-pound loads. Only Tenzing and three other porters would have the strength and skill to go to the high camps near the summit.

It Takes a Team

For each level that the climbers reached, a higher degree of teamwork was required. One set of men would exhaust themselves just to get equipment up the mountain for the next group. Two-man teams would work their way up the mountain, finding a path, cutting steps, securing ropes. And then they would be finished, having spent themselves to make the next leg of the climb possible for another team. Of the teamwork involved, Tenzing remarked,

> You do not climb a mountain like Everest by trying to race ahead on your own, or by competing with your comrades. You do it slowly

> and carefully, by unselfish teamwork. Certainly I wanted to reach the top myself; it was the thing I had dreamed of all my life. But if the lot fell to someone else I would take it like a man, and not a cry-baby. For that is the mountain way.[3]

The team of climbers, using the "mountain way," ultimately made it possible for two pairs to make an attempt at reaching the summit. The first consisted of Tom Bourdillon and Charles Evans. When they tried and failed, the other team got its chance. That team consisted of Tenzing and Edmund Hillary. Tenzing wrote of the first team:

> They were worn-out, sick with exhaustion, and, of course, terribly disappointed that they had not reached the summit themselves. But still . . . they did everything they could to advise and help us. And I thought, Yes, that is how it is on a mountain. That is how a mountain makes men great. For where would Hillary and I have been without the others? Without the climbers who had made the route and the Sherpas who had carried the loads? Without Bourdillon and Evans, Hunt and Da Namgyal, who had cleared the way ahead? Without Lowe and Gregory, Ang Hyima, Ang Tempra, and Penba, who were there only to help us? It was only because of the work and sacrifice of all of them that we were now to have our chance at the top.[4]

They made the most of their chance. On May 29, 1953, Tenzing Norgay and Edmund Hillary accomplished what no other human being ever had: They stood on the summit of Mount Everest, the world's highest peak!

Could Tenzing and Hillary have made it alone? The answer is

no. Could they have made it without a great team? Again, the answer is no. Why? Because *as the challenge escalates, the need for teamwork elevates.* That's the Law of Mount Everest.

What Is Your Everest?

You may not be a mountain climber, and you may not have any desire to reach the summit of Everest. But I bet you have a dream. I say that with confidence because deep down everybody has one—even the people who haven't figured out what theirs is yet. If you have a dream, you need a team to accomplish it.

How do you approach the task of putting together a team to accomplish your dream? I think the best way to start is to ask yourself three questions:

1. "What Is My Dream?"

It all starts with this question because your answer reveals *what could be.* Robert Greenleaf remarked, "Nothing much happens without a dream. For something really great to happen, it takes a really great dream."

What lies in your heart? What do you see as a possibility for your life? What would you like to accomplish during your time on this earth? Only a dream will tell you such things. As Harlem Renaissance poet Langston Hughes wrote:

> Hold fast to dreams for if dreams die,
> Life is a broken-winged bird that cannot fly.
> Hold fast to dreams for when dreams go,
> Life is a barren field frozen with snow.

If you want to do something great, you must have a dream. But a dream is not enough. You can fulfill a dream only if you are part of a team.

2. "Who Is on My Team?"

This second question tells you *what is*. It measures your current situation. Your potential is only as good as your current team. That's why you must examine who is joining you on your journey. A mountain climber like Maurice Wilson, who had only three halfhearted companions, was never able to accomplish his dream of climbing the mountain. However, someone like Tenzing Norgay, who always climbed Everest with the best mountaineers in the world, was able to make it to the top. A great dream with a bad team is nothing more than a nightmare.

3. "What Should My Dream Team Look Like?"

The truth is that your team must be the size of your dream. If it's not, then you won't achieve it. You simply cannot achieve an ultimate number ten dream with a number four team. It just doesn't happen. If you want to climb Mount Everest, you need a Mount Everest–sized team. There's no other way to do it. It's better to have a great team with a weak dream than a great dream with a weak team.

> *Your team must be the size of your dream.*

Focus on the Team, Not the Dream

One mistake I've seen people repeatedly make is that they focus too much attention on their dream and too little on their team. But the truth is that if you build the right team, the dream will almost take care of itself.

> *Many people focus too much attention on their dream and too little on their team.*

Every dream brings challenges of its own. The kind of challenge determines the kind of team you need to build. Consider a few examples:

Type of Challenge	*Type of Team Required*
New Challenge	Creative Team
Controversial Challenge	United Team
Changing Challenge	Fast and Flexible Team
Unpleasant Challenge	Motivated Team
Diversified Challenge	Complementary Team
Long-term Challenge	Determined Team
Everest-sized Challenge	Experienced Team

If you want to achieve your dream—I mean really do it, not just imagine what it would be like—then grow your team. But as you do so, make sure your motives are right. Some people gather a team just to benefit themselves. Others do it because they enjoy the team experience and want to create a sense of community. Still others do it because they want to build an organization. The funny thing about these reasons is that if you're motivated by *all* of them, then your desire to build a team probably comes from wanting to add value to everyone on the team. But if your desire to build the team comes as the result of only one of these reasons, you probably need to examine your motives.

How to Grow a Team

When the team you have doesn't match up to the team of your dreams, then you have only two choices: Give up your dream, or grow up your team. Here is my recommendation concerning how to do the latter.

> *When the team you have doesn't match up to the team of your dreams, then you have only two choices: Give up your dream, or grow up your team.*

1. Develop Team Members

The first step to take with a team that's not realizing its potential is to help individual team members to grow. If you're leading the team, then one of your most important responsibilities is to see the potential that people don't see in themselves and draw it out. When you accomplish this, you're doing your job as a leader.

Think about the people on your team, and determine what they need based on the following categories:

- Enthusiastic beginner—needs direction
- Disillusioned learner—needs coaching
- Cautious completer—needs support
- Self-reliant achiever—needs responsibility

Always give the people who are already on your team a chance to grow and bloom. That's what early British explorer Eric Shipton did with a young, inexperienced kid named Tenzing in 1935, and his country was rewarded eighteen years later with a successful climb of the world's highest peak.

2. Add Key Team Members

Even if you give every person on your team a chance to learn and grow, and all of them make the most of the opportunities, you may find that you still lack the talent needed to accomplish your dream. That's when it's time to recruit that talent. Sometimes all the team needs is one key person with talent in an area to make the difference between success and failure. (I'll talk more about this in the Law of the Bench.)

3. Change the Leadership

Various team challenges require different kinds of leadership. If a team has the right talent but still isn't growing, sometimes the best thing you can do is to ask someone from the team who has previously been a follower to step into a leadership role. That transition may occur only for a short season, or it may be more permanent.

> *The challenge of the moment often determines the leader for that challenge.*

The challenge of the moment often determines the leader for that challenge. Why? Because every person on the team has strengths and weaknesses that come into play. That was the case for the Everest team as they faced every stage of the journey. Colonel Hunt chose the climbers and led the expedition, casting vision, modeling unselfish service, and making critical decisions about who would take which part. Tenzing chose the porters, leading, organizing, and motivating them to build the camps at each stage of the mountain. And the climbing teams took turns leading, cutting the trail up the mountain so that Hillary and Tenzing could make the final climb to the summit. When a particular challenge emerged, so did a leader to meet it. And everyone worked together, doing his part.

If your team is facing a big challenge, and it doesn't seem to be making any progress "up the mountain," then it might be time to change leaders. There may be someone on the team more capable for leading during this season. (Learn more by reading the myths of the head table and the round table in the Law of the Edge.)

4. Remove Ineffective Members

Sometimes a team member can turn a winning team into a losing one, either through lack of skill or a poor attitude. In those cases you must put the team first and make changes for the greater good.

Tenzing faced that situation during the Everest expedition of 1953. During early days of travel, there were continual flare-ups between the porters and the British team of climbers, and as sirdar, Tenzing was constantly stuck in the middle trying to work things out. After repeatedly negotiating the peace between the two parties, Tenzing discovered that the source of the problem was two Sherpas who were stirring up dissension. He promptly fired them and sent them home. Peace was quickly restored. If your team keeps breaking down or falling short, you may need to make changes in your team.

Growing a team is demanding and time-consuming. But if you want to achieve your dream, you have no other choice. The greater the dream, the greater the team. *As the challenge escalates, the need for teamwork elevates.* That is the Law of Mount Everest.

NOT EVERY CHALLENGE IS A DREAM

The challenges that our teams face are not always ones we select. Sometimes they are thrust upon us, and we have no choice but to do the best we can with the team we have, or give up and suffer the consequences. That was certainly the case for the crew and support team for Apollo 13.

If you saw the movie *Apollo 13* starring Tom Hanks (or remember some of the coverage on television during the actual flight as I do), then you know the basic story. On April 13, 1970, at 10:07 P.M. EST, an oxygen tank in the service module of the *Odyssey* spacecraft exploded, causing the ship to lose its oxygen supply and all normal power. In addition, the ship's main engine was rendered nonfunctional. Since the ship was 200,000 miles away from earth and on a course that would put it into a permanent orbit around the moon, it was a potentially disastrous—and possibly fatal—challenge.

The astronauts in the *Odyssey*, James Lovell, John Swigart Jr., and Fred Haise, would not be able to make it back to earth on their own. Their survival depended on teamwork at a level that the space program had never experienced—and it was used to having people work together like a well-oiled machine.

Teamwork at a New Level

The flight control team on the ground immediately instructed the command crew to shut down the ailing command capsule and move into the lunar module (LM) *Aquarius* for their safety. That put the crew out of harm's way for the moment. But they still faced two major challenges:

1. Getting the command module, *Odyssey*, and the lunar module, *Aquarius*, on the quickest course home.

2. Conserving the "consumables" that kept the astronauts alive: power, oxygen, and water.

Accomplishing both would severely test everyone's abilities and know-how.

During a typical Apollo mission, Houston's mission control employed four teams of controllers, each designated by a color: white, black, gold, and maroon. Each team had technicians responsible for various specific areas required to keep the ship on course. The usual procedure was for each team to take a six-hour shift under the guidance of one of three flight directors. But with the lives of three astronauts on the line, every member of every team jumped in to help. And one team was pulled from the usual rotation by Gene Kranz, the lead flight director, and dubbed the Tiger Team. Those fifteen men worked as a crisis management team.

As Kranz gathered them together, he told them,

> For the rest of the mission, I'm pulling you men off console. The people out in that room [the other teams] will be running the flight from moment to moment, but it's the people in this room who will be coming up with the protocols they're going to be executing . . . For the next few days we're going to be coming up with techniques and maneuvers we've never tried before. I want to make sure we know what we're doing.[5]

In addition, NASA promptly sent word out to contractor representatives, such as the people at Grumman Aerospace, who had built the lunar module. (And when word got out that there was trouble with Apollo 13, virtually *everyone* in the organization showed up at the facility in the middle of the night to pitch in.) They also pulled in every top specialist and experienced astronaut they had, quickly building a coast-to-coast network of simulators, computers, and experts. NASA records state:

> Astronauts Alan Shepard and Ed Mitchell operated one of the LM simulators at the Manned Spacecraft Center in Houston, and Gene Cernan and David Scott worked in the other. At Cape Kennedy, Astronaut Dick Gordon simulated emergency procedures in a third LM. One team of simulator specialists worked around the clock without a break. No procedure, no maneuver instruction, no checklist was relayed to the crew that hadn't been thoroughly proved out.[6]

As Easy As One, Two, Three

The team's first task was to figure out how to get the lunar module, which had been designed to support two men for 49.5 hours, to sustain three men for 84 hours. They did that by determining how to get the ship to run using the bare minimum number of systems, which would use less than one-fourth of its normal power.

Next, they had to get the spacecraft on a course that would return it to earth. That was no simple task since they would have to use the lunar module's tiny engine, and the guidance systems were off-line. But between the efforts of the crew, the expertise of the lunar module's manufacturer, and the calculations of Tiger Team, they were able to do it. And they also boosted the craft's speed to shorten the flight time. That would preserve precious water and energy.

The third major challenge the team faced was making the air that the crew was breathing safe. Oxygen was not a problem because the small lunar module was well supplied. But carbon dioxide was building up to dangerous levels because the small craft intended to land on the moon had not been designed to remove so much of it.

The crew on the ground worked out a clever way to adapt the lithium hydroxide filters from the command module so that they would work with the lunar module's noncompatible system.

Each time NASA's massive team faced an obstacle that threatened to leave the crew stranded in space, their pooled ingenuity, inherent tenacity, and incredible cooperation enabled them to overcome it. As a result, on April 17, 1970, the crew of the *Odyssey* made it safely home. NASA likes to call the mission a "successful failure." I call it a lesson in the Law of Mount Everest. *As the challenge escalates, the need for teamwork elevates.*

Putting men on the moon is an incredible challenge. But getting them home when things go wrong 200,000 miles away from earth is an even greater one. Fortunately for those men, the dream team was already in place when they got in trouble. And that is one of the lessons of Apollo 13. The time to build your team is not in the midst of a life-or-death challenge, but long before one can happen. If you haven't already, start building today so that when a formidable challenge occurs, you and your team will be ready.

Teamwork Thought

The size of your dream should determine the size of your team.

Becoming a Better Team Member

What is your natural first reaction when a challenge becomes more difficult? Do you go off alone to think? Do you try to solve the problem alone? Do you stay away from other people to avoid the pressure? Or do you lean on your teammates and let them lean on you?

If you don't already do it, teach yourself to rally with your teammates. You cannot win a great challenge alone. As Tenzing asserted, "On a great mountain, you do not leave your companions and go to the top alone."[7]

Becoming a Better Team Leader

What kinds of adjustments do you need to make to create your dream team, one that can meet the challenges ahead? Do you need to spend more time developing your people? Do you need to add key team members? Or should you make changes to the leadership? And don't forget that you, too, need to keep growing. What's true for a teammate is also true for the leader: If you don't grow, you gotta go.

COMPANION ONLINE RESOURCE

Learn more about how the Law of Mount Everest uniquely applies to you.

Take the FREE Law of Mount Everest assessment at **LawsOfTeamwork.com**.

5

THE LAW OF THE CHAIN

The Strength of the Team Is Impacted by Its Weakest Link

On March 24, 1989, the news broke that an environmental disaster had occurred in Alaska's Prince William Sound. The oil tanker *Exxon Valdez* had run aground on the Bligh Reef, damaging the hull of the ship and rupturing eight of the vessel's eleven cargo tanks. As a result, 10.8 million of the ship's approximately 53 million gallons of oil poured out of the ship and into the sea.

The negative impact on the area was immense. Fishing and tourism came to a halt, harming the local economy. The environment suffered. Experts estimate wildlife losses at 250,000 seabirds, 2,800 sea otters, 300 harbor seals, 250 bald eagles, 22 killer whales, and billions of eggs for food-fish species such as salmon and herring. Though it wasn't the largest oil spill on record, experts consider it to be the worst spill in history in terms of the damage done to the environment.[1]

Of course, Exxon, the company that owns the ship, also paid a price. The company's representatives estimate that the incident cost Exxon $3.5 *billion:*

- $2.2 billion in cleanup costs
- $300 million in claims paid
- $1 billion in state and federal settlements[2]

But that's not all. In addition to what Exxon has already paid, the company stands to lose an additional $5 billion in punitive damages, a judgment it is still attempting to reverse through the appellate process more than a decade after the incident. What was the cause of such an expensive and far-reaching accident? The answer can be found in the Law of the Chain.

The Broken Chain

When the *Exxon Valdez* cast off from the Alyeska Pipeline Terminal on the evening of March 23, the voyage began routinely. An expert ship's pilot guided the vessel through the Valdez Narrows and then returned control of the ship to its captain, Joe Hazelwood. The captain ordered that the ship be put on a particular course, turned control over to Third Mate Gregory Cousins, and left the bridge. Thirty-five minutes later, the *Exxon Valdez* was stranded on a reef and leaking tons of oil into the sea.

Investigation following the accident painted an ugly picture: neglect of safety standards, indifference to company policy, and unwise decision making. The ship's captain had been drinking in the hours before he took command of the ship. One officer, rather than the required two, remained in the wheelhouse as the tanker navigated the Valdez Narrows and again after the pilot left the ship. (And that officer, Cousins, had been so overworked that fatigue is thought to have contributed to the navigation error that followed.) Nor was a lookout always present on the bridge while the vessel was under way.

There were also discrepancies between what Captain Hazelwood told the Vessel Traffic Center he was doing and the orders he actually gave on the ship. At 11:30 P.M., the captain radioed that he would take a course of 200 degrees and reduce speed to wind his way through the icebergs that sometimes float in the shipping lanes. Yet the engine logs showed that the ship's speed kept increasing. Nine minutes after that, the captain ordered that the ship take a course of 180 degrees and be put on autopilot, but he never informed the traffic center of the change. Then at 11:53, he left the bridge.

At four minutes after midnight, the ship was on the reef. For almost two hours, first Cousins and then Hazelwood tried to get the ship free, all the while leaking oil into the sea. In the first three hours, it's estimated that 5.8 million gallons poured from the distressed tanker. By then, the damage was done, and the weak link had caused the "chain" to break. Alaska's coastline was a mess, Hazelwood's career as a ship's captain was over, and Exxon was stuck with a public relations nightmare—and massive financial obligations.

As much as any team likes to measure itself by its best people, the truth is that *the strength of the team is impacted by its weakest link.* No matter how much people try to rationalize it, compensate for it, or hide it, a weak link will eventually come to light. That's the Law of the Chain.

YOUR TEAM IS NOT FOR EVERYONE

One of the mistakes I often made early in my career as a team leader was that I thought everyone who was on my team should remain on the team. That was true for several reasons. First, I naturally see the best in people. When I look at individuals with potential, I see all that they can become—even if they don't see it. And I try to encourage and equip them to become better. Second, I truly like people. I figure the more who take the trip, the bigger the party. Third, because I have vision and believe my goals are worthwhile and beneficial, I sometimes naively assume that everyone will want to go along with me.

But just because I wanted to take everyone with me didn't mean that it would always work out that way. My first memorable experience with this occurred in 1980 when I was offered an executive position at Wesleyan World Headquarters in Marion, Indiana. When I accepted the position, I invited my assistant to come with me to be a part of the new team I was building. So she and her husband considered my offer and went to Marion to look around. I'll never forget when they came back. As I excitedly talked about the coming challenges and how we could begin to tackle them, I began to realize from the expressions on their faces that something was wrong. And that's when they told me. They weren't going.

That statement took me completely by surprise. In fact, I was sure that they were making a mistake and told them so, doing my best to convince them to change their minds. But my wife, Margaret, gave me some very good advice. She said, "John, your problem is that you want to take everybody with you. But not everyone is going to go on the journey. Let it go." It was a hard lesson for me to learn—and sometimes it still is.

From that experience and others I've had since then, I've discovered that when it comes to teamwork . . .

1. Not Everyone Will Take the Journey

Some people don't want to go. My assistant and her husband wanted to stay in Lancaster, Ohio, where they had built relationships for many years. For other people the issue is their attitude. They don't want to change, grow, or conquer new territory. They hold fast to the status quo. All you can do with people in this group is kindly thank them for their past contributions and move on.

2. Not Everyone Should Take the Journey

Other people shouldn't join a team because it's a matter of their agenda. They have other plans, and where you're going isn't the right place for them. The best thing you can do for people in this category is wish them well, and as far as you are able, help them on their way so that they achieve success in their venture.

3. Not Everyone Can Take the Journey

For the third group of people, the issue is ability. They may not be capable of keeping pace with their teammates or helping the group get where it wants to go. How do you recognize people who fall into this category? They're not very hard to identify.

- They can't keep pace with other team members.
- They don't grow in their area of responsibility.
- They don't see the big picture.
- They won't work on personal weaknesses.
- They won't work with the rest of the team.
- They can't fulfill expectations for their area.

If you have people who display one or more of those characteristics, then you need to acknowledge that they are weak links.

That's not to say that they are necessarily bad people. In fact, some teams exist to serve weak links or help them become stronger. It depends on the team's goals. For example, when I was a senior pastor, we reached out to people in the community with food and assistance. We helped people with addictions, divorce recovery, and many other difficulties. Our goal was to serve them. It's good and appropriate to help people who find themselves in those circumstances. But putting them on the team while they are still broken and weak doesn't help them, and it hurts the team—even to the extent of making the team incapable of accomplishing its goal of service.

What can you do with people on your team who are weak links? You really have only two choices: You need to train them or trade them. Of course, your first priority should always be to try to train people who are having a hard time keeping up. Help can come in many forms: giving people books to read, sending them to conferences, presenting them with new challenges, pairing them with mentors. I believe that people often rise to your level of expectations. Give them hope and training, and they usually improve.

But what should you do if a team member continually fails to meet expectations, even after receiving training, encouragement, and opportunities to grow? My father used to have a saying: "Water seeks its own level." Somebody who is a weak link on your team might be capable of becoming a star on another team. You need to give that person an opportunity to find his level somewhere else.

The Impact of a Weak Link

If you are a team leader, you cannot avoid dealing with weak links. Team members who don't carry their own weight slow down the team, and they have a negative effect on your leadership. Several things may happen when a weak link remains on the team:

1. The Stronger Members Identify the Weak One

A weak link cannot hide (except in a group of weak people). If you have strong people on your team, they always know who isn't performing up to the level of everyone else.

2. The Stronger Members Have to Help the Weak One

If your people must work together as a team to do their work, then they have only two choices when it comes to a weak teammate. They can ignore the person and allow the team to suffer, or they can help him and make the team more successful. If they are team players, they will help.

3. The Stronger Members Come to Resent the Weak One

Whether strong team members help or not, the result will always be the same: resentment. No one likes to lose or fall behind consistently because of the same person.

4. The Stronger Members Become Less Effective

Carrying someone else's load in addition to your own compromises your performance. Do that for a long time, and the whole team suffers.

5. The Stronger Members Question the Leader's Ability

Anytime the leader allows a weak link to remain a part of the team, the team members forced to compensate for the weak person begin to doubt the leader's courage and discernment. You lose the respect of the best when you don't deal properly with the worst.

> *You lose the respect of the best when you don't deal properly with the worst.*

Many team members may be able to avoid the hard decision of dealing with subpar members, but leaders can't. In fact, one of the differences between leaders and followers is action. Followers often know what to do, but they are unwilling or unable to follow through. But know this: If other people on the team make decisions for you because you are unwilling or unable to make them, then your leadership is being compromised, and you're not serving the team well.

Strengthening the Chain

Weak team members always take more of the team's time than strong ones. One reason is that the more competent people have to give their time to compensate for those who don't carry their share of the load. The greater the difference in competence between the more accomplished performers and the less accomplished ones, the greater the detriment to the team. For example, if you rate people on a scale from 1 to 10 (with 10 being the best), a 5 among 10s really hurts the team where an 8 among 10s often does not.

Let me show you how this works. When you first put together a group of people, their talents come together in a way that is analogous to addition. So visually a 5 among 10s looks like this:

$$10 + 10 + 10 + 10 + 5 = 45$$

The difference between this team and great ones with five 10s is like the difference between 50 and 45. That's a difference of 10 percent. But once a team comes together and starts to develop chemistry, synergy, and momentum, it's analogous to multiplication. That's when a weak link really starts to hurt the team. It's the difference between this:

10 x 10 x 10 x 10 x 10 = 100,000

and this:

10 x 10 x 10 x 10 x 5 = 50,000

That's a difference of 50 percent! The power and momentum of the team may be able to compensate for a weak link for a while, but not forever. A weak link eventually robs the team of momentum—and potential.

Ironically, weak links are less aware than stronger members of their weaknesses and shortcomings. They also spend more time guarding their turf, saving their positions, and holding on to what they have. And know this: When it comes to interaction between people, the weaker person usually controls the relationship. For example, someone with a good self-image is more flexible than a person with a poor self-image. An individual with a clear vision acts more readily than someone without one. A person with superb ability and high energy accomplishes more and works longer than an individual with lesser gifts. If the two people journey together, the stronger member must constantly work with and wait on the weaker one. That controls what happens on the journey.

If your team has a weak link who can't or won't rise to the level of the team—and you've done everything you can to help the person improve—then you've got to take action. When you do, heed the advice of authors Danny Cox and John Hoover. If you need to remove somebody from the team, be discreet, be clear, be honest, and be brief. Then once the person is gone, be open about it with the rest of the team while maintaining respect for the person you let go.[3] And if you start to have second thoughts before or afterward, remember this: As long as a weak link is part of the team, everyone else on the team will suffer.

No Weak Links!

Nobody particularly wants to have a weak link on a team, someone who causes the team to fail at its objectives. Yet we've all had to work with weaker team members. And sometimes good experiences have come out of it. There is rich personal reward to be reaped by helping a teammate go from being a weak link to a solid team member—and sometimes even to becoming a star player. But for good or bad, dealing with subpar performers is an inevitable part of being on any team, right? There's no such thing as a team that has no weak links, is there?

As I already mentioned, the goal of the team often determines how well it can work with a weak link. Sometimes the stakes for a team are so high that its members cannot afford to have a weak link. And that is the case for the U.S. Navy SEALs. The jobs they do are so demanding that a weak person on the team will get everyone on the team killed.

In recent years the SEALs have generated a lot of popular interest. They've been the subject of numerous novels and movies. They've captured people's imaginations because they are considered the best of the best. As one former SEAL remarked, "No group of men is closer to perfection in their chosen field."

The SEALs were first commissioned by President John F. Kennedy in 1962. They evolved from the underwater demolition teams who were developed during World War II to clear the amphibious landing areas of obstacles in such locations as Omaha and Utah Beaches in Normandy and later on the islands of the Pacific. Like all the special operations forces in the various branches of the U.S. military, they are experts in weapons, hand-to-hand combat, and demolition, and they have trained to parachute from airplanes. But their expertise is in operations based on and in water. That's the origin of their name: SEALs indicates that they are capable of operating in the **SE**a, from the **A**ir, and on **L**and.

FORGING THE CHAIN

The key to the success of the SEALs is their training—the real emphasis of which is not learning about weapons or gaining technical skills; it's about strengthening people and developing teamwork. Weapons change, and so do methods of conducting operations, but the intense mental and physical training has remained much the same for all the years that the SEALs have been in existence. Peter J. Schoomaker, commander in chief of U.S. Special Operations Command, says, "Everything but our core values are on the table; we have to be ready to change anything but those values to get the job done. The core value for a SEAL Team is the people."[4]

Having the right people on the team starts with the selection process. Only a certain kind of person will even apply to go through SEAL training. And of those who apply, only one in ten is accepted. (The navy recommends that candidates be running at least thirty miles a week and swimming long distances *before* they apply.) Those who do make it into the program then undergo twenty-six weeks of intense physical, psychological, and mental stress. The physical and emotional rigors of that training make marine boot camp look like a picnic. John Roat, who went through the training, was one of the first members of the newly formed SEAL teams in 1962. He said that more than 1,300 men tested to get into the training, but the program accepted only 134. The bar for physical training was so high that people began dropping out the first day. And he saw that as a good thing. He explained:

> There were still some 130 guys when the instructors broke us up into ten-man boat crews and gave us our boats . . . The men of each crew carried their boat on their heads, and until a crew got its ducks in a row, everyone in it suffered. There was no chance of a boat crew's learning how to work as a team until it got rid of the men who didn't belong in training. Until they were gone, they were just an added harassment factor. Sounds cold, but that's life.[5]

For the first five weeks, the training is torturous and the physical demands incredible. Then comes Hell Week, five days of constant physical and mental challenges where the trainees are kept awake and training for all but four or five hours during the entire week. It's the trial that eliminates remaining weak links and at the same time forges the class into a real team. Roat described the impact of that part of the training:

> Each training class still learns the same things during Hell Week: You can go farther than you ever thought possible, but you can't do it alone, and everyone left standing belongs there. Hell Week has changed less than any part of training, for one simple reason: The instructors cannot find a better way. You can't pick the ones who can

> hack it by their looks. No written test will find out if a man is a Team player. If it was possible to get good operators by letting some shrink interview trainees and say yea or nay, the navy would love it. The big problem is, the psychologists can't predict who will survive five-plus days of no sleep, with constant harassment, and impossible physical demands with an easy way out. That's still the test.[6]

SEAL training is so intense that there have been classes from which *no one* completed the training. In the end, 49 of the 134 people who started training with Roat graduated. The hearts of those who made it through the stress and pain can be represented by the words of one of Roat's classmates: "I couldn't quit; I would have let my classmates down. I just couldn't do it."

Many people consider the Navy SEALs to be the elite among the already elite company of special operations forces in the U.S. military. Their interaction is the definition of teamwork, and they depend upon each other at a level that most people cannot understand and will never experience. Their survival depends on it. And for that reason, they cannot afford to have any weak links.

Although you may never have to face the pressures that SEALs do, you can be sure of this: *The strength of the team is impacted by its weakest link.* No matter what kind of team you're on, that's always true. That's the Law of the Chain.

TEAMWORK THOUGHT

The team cannot continually cover up its weakness.

Becoming a Better Team Member

Most people's natural inclination is to judge themselves according to their best qualities while they measure others by their worst. As a result, they point to areas where their teammates need to grow. But the truth is that every person is responsible for his own growth first.

Take a hard look at yourself. Using the criteria from the chapter, examine yourself to see where you may be hindering the team. Mark the box under the word *Self* for any issue that applies to you. And if you have real courage, ask your spouse or a close friend to evaluate you by marking the boxes listed under the word *Friend.*

Evaluated by *Self*	*Friend*	**Possible Issues**
❑	❑	*Have trouble keeping pace with other team members.*
❑	❑	*Am not growing in my area of responsibility.*
❑	❑	*Have a hard time seeing the big picture.*
❑	❑	*Have difficulty seeing my personal weakness.*
❑	❑	*Have a tough time working with the rest of the team.*
❑	❑	*Consistently fail to fulfill expectations in area of responsibility.*

If you (or the other person who evaluated you) checked more than one box, you need to put yourself on a growth plan so that you don't hinder your team. Talk to your team leader or a trusted mentor about ways you can grow in any weak area.

Becoming a Better Team Leader

If you're a team leader, you cannot ignore the issues created by a weak link. For the various kinds of teams, different solutions are appropriate. If the team is a family, then you don't simply "trade" weak people. You lovingly nurture them and try to help them grow, but you also try to minimize the damage they can cause to other family members. If the team is a business, then you have responsibilities to the owner or stockholders. If you've offered training without success, then a "trade" might be in order. If the team is a ministry and training has made no impact, then it might be appropriate to ask the weak people to sit on the sidelines for a while. Or they might need some time away from the team to work on emotional or spiritual issues.

No matter what kind of situation you face, remember that your responsibilities to people come in the following order: to the organization, to the team, and then to the individual. Your own interests—and comfort—come last.

COMPANION
ONLINE
RESOURCE

Learn more about how the Law of the Chain uniquely applies to you.

Take the FREE Law of the Chain assessment at **LawsOfTeamwork.com**.

6

THE LAW OF THE CATALYST

Winning Teams Have Players Who Make Things Happen

Most teams don't naturally get better on their own. Left alone, they don't grow, improve, and reach championship caliber. Instead, they tend to wind down. The road to the next level is always uphill, and if a team isn't intentionally fighting to move up, then it inevitably slides down. The team loses focus, gets out of rhythm, decreases in energy, breaks down in unity, and loses momentum. At some point, it also loses key players. And it's only a matter of time before it plateaus and ultimately declines into mediocrity. That's why a team that reaches its potential always possesses a catalyst.

> *Catalysts are get-it-done-and-then-some people.*

The Definition of a Catalyst

Catalysts are what I call get-it-done-and-then-some people. The most outstanding one I've ever had the privilege of seeing in action is Michael Jordan. In the opinion of many people (including me), he is the greatest basketball player ever to play the game, not only because of his talent, athleticism, and understanding of the game, but also because of his ability as a catalyst. His résumé as an amateur, and as a professional with the Chicago Bulls attests to that ability:

- Won NCAA Division I Championship (1982)
- Named the *Sporting News* College Player of the Year twice (1983, 1984)
- Received the Naismith and Wooden Awards (1984)
- Won 2 Olympic gold medals (1984, 1992)
- Won 6 NBA world championships (1991, 1992, 1993, 1996, 1997, 1998)
- Selected NBA Rookie of the Year (1985)
- Selected to the NBA All-Rookie Team (1985)
- Selected for All-NBA First Team a record 10 times (1987, 1988, 1989, 1990, 1991, 1992, 1993, 1996, 1997, 1998)
- Holds the NBA record for highest career scoring average (31.5 points per game)
- Holds the NBA record for most seasons leading the league in scoring (10)
- Holds the NBA record for most seasons leading the league in field goals made (10) and attempted (10)

- Ranks 3rd in NBA history in points (29,277), 3rd in steals (2,306), and 4th in field goals made (10,962)
- Voted NBA Defensive Player of the Year (1985; after being criticized that he was "only" an offensive player)
- Selected to the All-NBA Defensive First Team 8 times (1988, 1989, 1990, 1991, 1993, 1997, 1998)
- Named NBA MVP 5 times (1988, 1991, 1992, 1996, 1998)
- Named NBA Finals MVP 6 times (1991, 1992, 1993, 1996, 1997, 1998)
- Named 1 of the 50 greatest players in NBA history

Statistics make a strong statement about Jordan, but they really don't tell the whole story. For that, you had to see him in action. When the Bulls needed to get the team out of a slump, the ball went to Jordan. When a player needed to take the last shot to win the game, the ball went to Jordan. Even if the team needed to get things going in practice, the ball went to Jordan. No matter what the situation was on the court, Jordan was capable of putting the team in the position to win the game. That's always the case for championship teams. *Winning teams have players who make things happen.* That's the Law of the Catalyst.

Still Making Things Happen

As you know, Michael Jordan has retired from basketball as a player. But he is still in the game. In early 2000, Jordan became part owner and president of basketball operations of the Washington Wizards. Only a week after becoming part of the organization, Jordan put on a number 23 Wizards jersey and joined the team for a practice.

Wizards forward Tracy Murray, who guarded Jordan during some drills, remarked afterward, "He's definitely moving the same way . . . dunking the ball, shooting a jump shot, fade away. Still got the same game, hasn't gone anywhere."

Nobody expected his talent to be diminished, especially not just two years after his retirement. But his ability as a catalyst hadn't diminished either. Murray continued, "And as soon as he sets foot in that gym, he starts talking trash, so of course the intensity is going to pick up."

Every catalyst brings intensity to the table. One commentator remarked of Jordan's visit to the court, "By being himself, he turned a Wizards practice into something it hasn't been in a while—energetic and fun."

"Which is what we should expect every day," was Jordan's reaction. "Actually, I told them they shouldn't have to wait for me to come out to show the energy that they had today. I just tried to keep them focused, challenge them, say whatever I have to say. If they can play hard against me, they can play hard against anybody. It was fun."[1]

That's the way it always is for a catalyst. Having fun. He loves stirring up the team, making things happen, doing whatever it takes to push the team to the next level. When a catalyst does that consistently, the team becomes expectant, confident, elevated, and ultimately amazed. That's the Law of the Catalyst. *Winning teams have players who make things happen!*

Three Kinds of Players

When crunch time comes, a catalyst becomes critical, whether it's the salesperson who hits the impossible goal, the ballplayer who makes the big play, or the parent who gets a child to believe in himself at a critical moment in life. A team can't reach big goals or even break new ground if it doesn't have a catalyst.

My experience with teams has taught me that what is true for sports is also the case for business, ministry, and family relationships. When the clock is running down and the game is on the line, there are really only three kinds of people on a team:

1. People Who Don't Want the Ball

Some people don't have the ability to come through for the team in high-pressure situations, and they know it. As a result, they don't want the responsibility of carrying the team to victory. And it shouldn't be given to them. They should be allowed to play in their areas of strength.

2. People Who Want the Ball But Shouldn't

A second group contains people who can't carry the team to victory. The problem is that *they don't know* that they can't. Often the cause is that these players' egos are greater than their talent. These people can be dangerous to a team.

3. People Who Want the Ball and Should

The final group, which is by far the smallest, consists of people who want to be "go to" players at crunch time and who can actually deliver. They are able to push, pull, or carry the team to new levels when the going gets tough. They are the catalysts.

Every team needs catalysts if it wants to have any hope of winning consistently. Without them, even a team with loads of talent cannot go to the highest level. I saw an illustration of this in the late 1990s and again in 2000 with the Atlanta Braves. They had the best starting pitchers in baseball. They had strong hitters, Gold Glove fielders, and talent in the bull pen. They possessed team members who had been league MVP or rookie of the year. But they lacked the catalytic players they needed to become World Series champions.

Characteristics of a Catalyst

It's easy to point out a team's catalyst after he has made an impact on the group and spurred the members on to victory, especially in the world of sports. You can point to particular moments when the person went to a whole new level and took the team there at the same time. But how do you recognize a catalyst *before* the fact? How do you look for catalytic people for your current team?

No matter what kind of "game" you're playing or what kind of team you're on, you can be sure that catalysts have certain characteristics that make them different from their teammates. I've observed that these nine are often present in the catalysts with whom I've interacted. They are . . .

1. Intuitive

Catalysts sense things that others don't sense. They may recognize a weakness in an opponent. They may be able to make an intuitive leap that turns a disadvantage into an advantage. They are able to use whatever it is they sense to help the team succeed.

For different kinds of teams, the way the intuition plays out changes. That makes sense because the goal of the team determines what the team values. Another reason is that people are most intuitive in their areas of natural strength. So for a small business, the catalyst may be an entrepreneur who can smell an opportunity when no one else is aware of it. For a ministry or other nonprofit organization, the catalyst may be a person who intuitively recognizes leadership and can recruit talented volunteers. For a football team, it may be a quarterback who senses that a defense isn't adjusting well and calls the play that wins the game. In each case the situation is different, but the result is the same: A catalyst senses an opportunity, and as a result, the team benefits.

2. *Communicative*

Catalysts say things that other team members don't say in order to get the team moving. Sometimes they do it to share with their teammates what they have sensed intuitively so that they will be better prepared to meet the challenge. Other times their purpose is to inspire or incite other team members. And they usually know the difference between when a teammate needs a boost—and when he needs a boot.

Anytime you see a team of people suddenly turn around or crank their play up to another level, you'll see someone on the team talking, directing, inspiring others. You'll see it, too, with strong political leaders. People such as Churchill, Roosevelt, and Kennedy changed the world with their words. They were catalysts, and catalysts communicate.

3. *Passionate*

Catalysts feel things that others don't feel. They are passionate about what they do, and they want to share that love with their teammates. Sometimes the passion explodes as a controlled fury to achieve goals in their area of passion. Other times it manifests itself as a contagious enthusiasm. But however it comes out, it can inspire a team to success.

Legendary baseball player Pete Rose of the Cincinnati Reds has experienced his share of problems, but he was certainly one of the great catalysts of his sport in the twentieth century. He was once asked which goes first on a baseball player: his eyes, his legs, or his arm. Rose's response was telling. He said, "None of these things. It's when his enthusiasm goes that he's through as a player." And he's also through as a catalyst.

4. Talented

Catalysts are capable of doing what others cannot do because their talent is as strong as their passion. People rarely become catalysts outside an area of expertise and gifting. That's the case for two main reasons. First, talent knows what it takes to win. You can't take the team to the next level when you haven't mastered the skills it takes to succeed on a personal level. It just doesn't happen.

The second reason people must have talent in an area where they desire to be a catalyst is that part of being a catalyst is influencing other team members. You can't do that if you have no credibility with them because of your own poor performance. Part of being a catalyst is sharing your gift with others to make them better. You can't give what you don't have.

5. Creative

Another quality commonly found in catalysts is creativity. Catalysts think things that others do not think. While most team members may do things by rote (or by rut), catalysts think differently from their teammates. They are constantly looking for fresh, innovative ways to do things.

Business and sports team consultant Carl Mays asserts that "creativity involves taking what you have, where you are, and getting the most out of it." Sometimes what they come up with can change the tempo of a game. Other times their ability to rewrite the rules changes the whole way the game is actually played.

6. Initiating

I enjoy creative people, and I've worked with many through the years. In fact, I consider myself to be creative, especially in the areas of writing and teaching. But my experience with creative people has taught me something about them: While all creative people have more than enough ideas, not all of them are good at implementing those creative thoughts.

Catalysts don't have this problem. They do things that others cannot do. Not only are they creative in their thinking, but they are disciplined in their actions. They delight in making things happen. That initiative can take almost any form: a baseball manager arguing with an umpire to stir up his players, a parent changing jobs or moving the family to help a struggling child, or a business owner putting up financial incentives for employees to break through barriers. So they initiate. And as a result they move the team as they move themselves.

7. Responsible

Catalysts carry things that others do not carry. My friend Truett Cathy, the founder of Chick-Fil-A, has a saying: "If it's to be, it's up to me." That could very well be the motto for all catalysts.

Not long ago a commercial appeared on television that showed a pair of consultants giving a company's CEO advice on how he could take his business to the next level. They explained how the company's computer system should be overhauled, how the distribution system could be improved, and how marketing channels could be changed to make the company much more effective and profitable.

The CEO listened carefully to everything they had to say, and finally he smiled and said, "I like it. Okay, do it."

The consultants looked confused for a moment, and one of them stammered, "We don't actually *do* what we recommend."

Catalysts are not consultants. They don't recommend a course of action. They take responsibility for making it happen.

8. Generous

Catalysts give things that others don't give. A true mark of people's taking responsibility is their willingness to give of themselves to carry something through. Catalysts display that quality. They are prepared to use their resources to better the team, whether that means giving time, spending money, or sacrificing personal gain.

> *Catalysts are not consultants. They don't recommend a course of action. They take responsibility for making it happen.*

A vivid example of someone giving of himself for the team can be found in the life of New York businessman Eugene Lang. On June 25, 1981, Lang stood before sixty-one graduating sixth graders in P.S. 121, the East Harlem elementary school from which he had graduated decades before. He knew that statistically, 75 percent of the children would probably drop out of school during the next six years and would never graduate from high school. And he wanted to try to do something to change that.

He began by encouraging them to work hard, telling them that if they did, success would follow. But then on the spur of the moment, Lang moved from consultant to catalyst. He promised those kids that if they would stick with it and graduate from high school, he would provide each of them with scholarship money for college. That promise was the start of what became the "I Have a Dream" program.

Four years later, all 61 students were still in school. Six years later, 90 percent of the 54 kids who remained in touch with Lang graduated from high school, and two-thirds of them went on to college. Today, I Have a Dream sponsors 160 projects in 57 cities, and it touches the lives of 10,000 kids—all because Lang decided to become a catalyst.[2]

9. Influential

Catalysts are able to lead teammates in a way that others cannot. Team members will follow a catalyst when they won't respond to anyone else. In the case of a highly talented team member who is not especially gifted in leadership, he may be an effective catalyst in an area of expertise. But people with natural leadership ability will have influence far beyond their own team.

Michael Jordan, once again, is a wonderful example. Obviously he had influence with his teammates in Chicago. But his influence stretched far beyond the Bulls. I got a taste of that firsthand at the NBA 2001 All-Star Game. I had the pleasure of speaking at the chapel for players and officials before the game, and later I got to spend time with the referees who had been picked to officiate. During my talks with them, I asked what player they respected the most in terms of his honesty. Their answer was Michael Jordan.

One ref then recounted that in a close game, Danny Ainge, whose team was playing against the Bulls, made a shot near the three-point line. The officials had given Ainge only two points for the basket since they were not sure whether he was outside the three-point line. During the timeout immediately after the shot, one of the refs asked Jordan whether his opponent's score had been a valid three-point shot. Jordan indicated that it was. They gave Ainge the three points. Jordan's integrity—and influence—caused them to reverse their call.

When you see many of those nine qualities in someone on your team, then take heart. When crunch time comes, he is likely to step up to a whole new level of performance and attempt to take the team there too.

My Own Go-to Guy

At my company, The INJOY Group, a number of team members are catalysts within the organization. But none are stronger than Dave Sutherland, the CEO.

Dave came on board in 1994 as the president of ISS, the division of The INJOY Group that helps churches with fund-raising through capital campaigns. Just prior to his coming on board, I had given serious thought to shutting down that arm of the organization. ISS wasn't supporting itself financially, it was draining time and resources from other more productive areas of the company, and it wasn't having the positive influence I had hoped for. But I believed that Dave Sutherland's leadership could make a difference. And soon after I hired him, I began seeing progress at ISS.

The second year that Dave was with me, the company had some pretty aggressive goals. That year the company's goal had been to partner with eighty churches, more than twice as many as it had the previous year. And each partnership could come only after a personal presentation to a church's board and their acceptance of our offer to help.

One day during the first week of December, I stopped by Dave's office and spoke to his wife, Roxine, who works with Dave as his assistant. I hadn't seen Dave in a while, and I asked where he was.

"He's on the road making a presentation," she said.

I thought that was a little odd because the company had several key people whose job it was to make the presentations to churches.

"On the road? When will he be back?" I asked.

"Well, let's see," said Roxine, "when he left the Monday after Thanksgiving, we still needed twenty-four more churches to reach our goal. Dave said he won't be home until we reach it."

And reach it he did. Dave was on the road until December 19. But that was no great surprise. My writer, Charlie Wetzel, told me that in a sales and marketing career that spans three decades, Dave has *never* missed a goal. Not once.

His tenacity and ability serve Dave well. But they also serve the team well. By reaching that goal, Dave made every person on the team a winner that year. And everyone in the company used the momentum he created to take ISS to a whole new level. A year later, ISS became the second largest company of its type in the world. And by the end of the year 2000, it had helped more than one thousand churches across America raise more than $1 billion.

When you have a Michael Jordan or a Eugene Lang or a Dave Sutherland, your team always has a chance to win. They are get-it-done-and-then-some people. Why is that important? Because *winning teams have players who make things happen.* Without them, a team will never reach its potential. That is the truth of the Law of the Catalyst.

Teamwork Thought

Games are won by get-it-done-and-then-some people.

Becoming a Better Team Member

How are you when it comes to crunch time on your team? Do you want the ball, or would you rather it was in someone else's hands? If there are more talented and effective catalysts on your team, then you should not want to be the go-to player in a pinch. In those cases, the best thing you can do is get an "assist" by helping to put those people into position to benefit the team. But if you avoid the spotlight because you are afraid or because you haven't worked as hard as you should to improve yourself, then you need to change your mind-set.

Start to put yourself on the road to improvement by doing the following things:

1. *Find a mentor.* Players become catalysts only with the help of people better than themselves. Find someone who makes things happen to help you along the way.

2. *Begin a growth plan.* Put yourself on a program that will help you develop your skills and talents. You cannot take the team to a higher level if you haven't gotten there.

3. *Get out of your comfort zone.* You won't know what you're capable of until you try to go beyond what you've done before.

If you follow these three guidelines, you still may not become a catalyst, but you will at least become the best you can be—and that's all that anyone can ask of you.

Becoming a Better Team Leader

If you lead a team, you need catalysts to push the team to its potential. Use the list of qualities in the chapter to begin identifying and enlisting people who can get it done and then some. If you see that potential in some of your current teammates, encourage them to take initiative and become positive influencers on the team. If the people on the team can't or won't step up to that level of play, then start recruiting people from outside the team. No team can go to the highest level without a catalyst. *Winning teams have players who make things happen.*

COMPANION ONLINE RESOURCE

Learn more about how the Law of the Catalyst uniquely applies to you.

Take the FREE Law of the Catalyst assessment at **LawsOfTeamwork.com**.

7

THE LAW OF THE COMPASS

Vision Gives Team Members Direction and Confidence

For nearly a hundred years, IBM has been a rock of American business standing firm in a stream of competition. Even during the Great Depression of the 1930s, while thousands of companies were disappearing, IBM kept growing. The source of its strength was business and technological innovation.

Introducing Technology

For a half century, IBM continually broke ground in the area of computers, beginning in the 1940s with its Mark I. In the 1950s and 1960s, the firm introduced innovation after innovation. By 1971, IBM was receiving $8 billion in annual revenues and employed 270,000 people. When people thought of blue-chip companies, IBM is likely the first one they pictured.

But for all its history of advances, by the late 1980s and early 1990s, the company was struggling. For a decade IBM had been slow to react to technological changes. As a result, by 1991, it suffered $8 billion in *losses* every year. And even though IBM fought to regain ground technologically, consumers' favorable perceptions of the company were at an all-time low. Where IBM had once been seen as dominant, people looked upon it as hopelessly behind the times—a slow-moving dinosaur among new companies that moved like cheetahs. If something didn't change, IBM was going to be in big trouble.

Then in 1993, IBM got a new CEO, Lou Gerstner. He quickly began recruiting key members for his team, IBM's executive committee. Perhaps the most important addition was Abby Kohnstamm, whom he invited to be IBM's senior vice president of marketing.

Introducing . . . a Compass

Kohnstamm was eager to get started. She believed the company's products were strong enough, but its marketing was weak. When she arrived at IBM, what she found was much worse than she had expected. Not only was IBM failing to reach customers effectively; when it came to the marketing department, employees weren't even sure who did what or why. For example, when Kohnstamm asked how many employees were in the marketing area, she couldn't get the same answer from any two employees. Greg Farrell of *USA Today* described the situation: "The company was a fragmented, decentralized organization with more than a dozen quasi-autonomous businesses, and 70 ad agency partners worldwide."[1]

Kohnstamm immediately dismissed all those agencies and hired one to replace it: Ogilvy & Mather Worldwide. Her desire was to give the entire IBM team a single unifying theme for the hardware, software, and services they had to offer. Before long, she had found it. The company adopted the concept of e-business. Kohnstamm asserts, "E-business is the single focal point for the company, and is the single largest marketing effort ever undertaken by IBM."[2]

The vision seems to be working. Steve Gardner, an ad agency owner who once promoted Compaq, says, "The most stunning thing about e-business was that it transformed IBM from perceived laggard to leader in the Internet space without any real change in its lines of products or services. That's an astonishing achievement."[3]

Where once IBM was struggling, it now has renewed direction and confidence. Bill Etherington, senior vice president and group executive over sales and distribution, notes that the marketing focus has had an incredibly positive effect on IBM's employees. And he should know. He's been with IBM for thirty-seven years. He says, "We all had enthusiasm for this wonderful campaign. It had an edge to it and portrayed the company in a much more modern light."[4] Maureen McGuire, vice president of marketing communications, agrees: "The campaign has galvanized employees. We're trying to get all those people to sing the same song, read from the same book." For a company that hadn't sung for a long time, that's a momentous achievement. And it just goes to show you, *vision gives team members direction and confidence.* That's the power of the Law of the Compass.

DON'T GET LOST

Have you ever been part of a team that didn't seem to make any progress? Maybe the group had plenty of talent, resources, and opportunities, and team members got along, but the group just never *went* anywhere! If you have, there's a strong possibility that the situation was caused by lack of vision.

Great vision precedes great achievement. Every team needs a compelling vision to give it direction. A team without vision is, at worst, purposeless. At best, it is subject to the personal (and sometimes selfish) agendas of its various teammates. As the agendas work against each other, the team's energy and drive drain away. On the other hand, a team that embraces a vision becomes focused, energized, and confident. It knows where it's headed and why it's going there.

> *Great vision precedes great achievement.*

Field Marshal Bernard Montgomery, a leader of troops during World War II who was called a "soldier's general," wrote that "every single soldier must know, before he goes into battle, how the little battle he is to fight fits into the larger picture, and how the success of his fighting will influence the battle as a whole." People on the team need to know why they're fighting. Otherwise, the team gets into trouble.

The Leader's Responsibility

Field Marshal Montgomery was adept at connecting with the soldiers on his team and casting vision for their battles. That ability brought him and them success. He understood that leaders must be vision casters. Author Ezra Earl Jones points out,

> Leaders do not have to be the greatest visionaries themselves. The vision may come from anyone. The leaders do have to state the

> vision, however. Leaders also have to keep the vision before the people and remind them of the progress that is being made to achieve the vision. Otherwise, the people might assume that they are failing and give up.

If you lead your team, then you are responsible for identifying a worthy and compelling vision and articulating it to your team members. However, even if you are not the leader, identifying a compelling vision is still important. If you don't know the team's vision, you can't perform with confidence. You can't be sure you and your teammates are going in the right direction. You can't even be sure that the team you're on is the right one for you if you haven't examined the vision in light of your strengths, convictions, and purpose. For everyone on the team, the vision needs to be compelling.

Check Your Compass!

How do you measure a vision? How do you know whether it is worthy and compelling? You check your compass. Every team needs one. In fact, every team needs several. A team should examine the following six "compasses" before embarking on any journey.

A team's vision must be aligned with:

1. A Moral Compass (Look Above)

Millionaire philanthropist Andrew Carnegie exclaimed, "A great business is seldom if ever built up, except on lines of strictest integrity." That holds true for any endeavor. There's only one true north. If your compass is pointing in any other direction, your team is headed the wrong way.

A moral compass brings integrity to the vision. It helps all the people on the team to check their motives and make sure that they are laboring for the right reasons. It also brings credibility to the leaders who cast the vision—but only if they model the values that the team is expected to embrace. When they do, they bring fuel to the vision, which keeps it going.

2. An Intuitive Compass (Look Within)

Where integrity brings fuel to the vision, passion brings fire. And the true fire of passion and conviction comes only from within.

In *The Leadership Challenge,* James Kouzes and Barry Posner explain that "visions spring forth from our intuition. If necessity is the mother of invention, intuition is the mother of vision. Experience feeds our intuition and enhances our insight." A vision must resonate deep within the leader of the team. Then it must resonate within the team members, who will be asked to work hard to bring it to fruition. But that's the value of intuitive passion. It brings the kind of heat that fires up the committed—and fries the uncommitted.

> *"A great business is seldom if ever built up, except on lines of strictest integrity."*
>
> —ANDREW CARNEGIE

3. A Historical Compass (Look Behind)

There's an old saying that I learned when I lived in rural Indiana: "Don't remove the fence before you know why it's there." You never know: There might be a bull on the other side! A compelling vision should build on the past, not diminish it. It should make positive use of anything contributed by previous teams in the organization.

Anytime you cast vision, you must create a connection between the past, the present, and the future. You must bring them together. People won't reach for the future until they have touched the past. When you include the history of the team, the people who have been in the organization a long time sense that they are valued (even if they are no longer the stars). At the same time, the newer people receive a sense of security, knowing that the current vision builds on the past and leads to the future.

People won't reach for the future until they have touched the past.

What is the best way to do that? You tell stories. Principles may fade in people's minds, but stories stick. They bring relationships to the vision. Tell stories from the past that give a sense of history. Tell stories about the exciting things that are happening now among team members. And tell the story of what it will be like the day that the team fulfills the vision. Stories are like thumbtacks that help to keep a vision in front of people.

4. A Directional Compass (Look Ahead)

Poet Henry David Thoreau wrote, "If one advances confidently in the direction of his dreams, and endeavors to live the life which he has imagined, he will meet with a success unexpected in common hours." As I already mentioned, vision provides direction for the team. Part of that direction comes from a sense of purpose. Another comes from having goals, which bring targets to the vision.

A goal motivates the team. NFL referee Jim Tunney commented on this when he said, "Why do we call it a goal line? Because eleven people on the offensive team huddle for a single purpose—to move the ball across it. Everyone has a specific task to do—the quarterback, the wide receiver, each lineman, every player knows exactly what his assignment is. Even the defensive team has its goals too—to prevent the offensive team from achieving its goal."

5. A Strategic Compass (Look Around)

A goal won't do the team much good without steps to accomplish it. Vision without strategy is little more than a daydream. As Vince Abner remarked, "Vision isn't enough—it must be combined with venture. It is not enough to stare up the steps; we must step up the stairs."

The value of a strategy is that it brings process to the vision. It identifies resources and mobilizes the members of the team. People need more than information and inspiration. They need instruction in what to do to make the vision become reality and a way to get there. A strategy provides that.

6. A Visionary Compass (Look Beyond)

The vision of the team must look beyond current circumstances and any obvious shortcomings of current teammates to see the potential of the team. A truly great vision speaks to what team members can become if they truly live out their values and work according to their highest standards.

If you are your team's leader, getting people to reach their potential means challenging them. As you know, it's one thing to have team members show up. It's another to get them to grow up. One of the things about having a far-reaching vision is that it brings "stretch" to the team.

> *"You must have a long-range vision to keep you from being frustrated by short-range failures."*
>
> —CHARLES NOBLE

Without a challenge many people tend to fall or fade away. Charles Noble observed, "You must have a long-range vision to keep you from being frustrated by short-range failures." That's true. Vision helps people with motivation. That can be especially important for highly talented people. They sometimes fight lack of desire. That's why a consummate artist like Michelangelo prayed, "Lord, grant that I may always desire more than I can accomplish." A visionary compass answers that prayer.

Someone said that only people who can see the invisible can do the impossible. That shows the value of vision. But it also indicates that vision can be an elusive quality. If you can confidently measure the vision of your team according to these six "compasses," and you find them all aligned in the right direction, then your team has a reasonably good chance at success. And make no mistake. Not only can a team fail to thrive without vision—it cannot even survive without it. The words of King Solomon of ancient Israel, reputed to be the wisest man who ever lived, are true: "Where there is no vision, the people perish."[5] *Vision gives team members direction and confidence,* two things they cannot do without. That is the critical nature of the Law of the Compass.

Coffee Magic

Some people capture a vision, as Abby Kohnstamm did at IBM, and they use it to focus their teams. Others are captured *by* a vision, and the power of it changes the courses of their lives.

That was certainly the case for Howard Schultz, the man who bought Starbucks Coffee Company in 1987.

Schultz was no stranger to Starbucks. In 1982, just six years out of Northern Michigan University, he had walked away from a great job as vice president in charge of U.S. operations at Hammarplast, a Swedish company that specializes in housewares, to join Starbucks. He had discovered the Seattle coffee retailer when he saw that their four stores sold more of Hammarplast's drip coffeemakers than Macy's in New York.

Schultz remembers the vision he had for Starbucks the day after his first visit to the company:

> It was like a shining jewel . . . There was something magic about it, a passion and authenticity I had never experienced in business. Maybe, just maybe, I could be part of that magic. Maybe I could help it grow. How would it feel to build a business? . . . How would it feel to own equity, not just collect a paycheck? What could I bring to Starbucks that could make it even better than it was?[6]

Schultz was captivated by a vision to expand Starbucks beyond Seattle, perhaps even across the entire country. When he began working for Starbucks as their director of retail operations and marketing, he started helping them to expand. But after Schultz had been with Starbucks for about a year, his vision for the coffee business itself also began to expand.

Make Mine a Grande!

After a visit to Italy, Schultz saw the huge potential of putting a coffee bar with espresso drinks in each Starbucks location. He believed that move held the greatest promise for the company, but he couldn't convince the owners to buy in to his vision. Since its inception in 1971, Starbucks had been a retailer of fresh whole coffee beans, not a seller of coffee by the cup.

Despite his love for Starbucks, Schultz left after three years to start his own company, which he made into a success. But two years later, when the owners of Starbucks let him know they wanted to sell the company, Schultz jumped at the chance. In 1987 the two companies merged and became the Starbucks Corporation.

Two factors drove Howard Schultz as he began the work of expanding Starbucks. The first was his love of coffee. The second was his desire to create a workplace that valued people and treated them with respect and dignity. That mattered to him greatly after a childhood of seeing his father struggle to support his family. Schultz says,

> I have a lot of respect for my dad. He never finished high school, but he was an honest man who worked hard. He sometimes had to take two or three jobs just to put food on the table. He cared a lot about his three kids, and played ball with us on weekends . . . But he was a beaten man. In a series of blue-collar jobs—truck driver, factory worker, cab driver—he never made as much as $20,000 a year, never could afford to own his own home. I spent my childhood in the Projects, federally subsidized housing in Canarsie, Brooklyn, [New York] . . . He had tried to fit into a system, but the system had crushed him.[7]

When it came to the coffee part of his vision, Schultz didn't worry about Starbucks. However, the working environment was another matter. In the two years he had been away from the company, the employees at Starbucks had become demoralized. Schultz says, "People were cynical and wary, beaten down and unappreciated. They felt abandoned by previous management and anxious about me. The fabric of trust and common vision that Starbucks had when I first joined had frayed badly."[8]

RECASTING THE VISION

Schultz began to address the issues immediately—starting with this statement to employees:

> Five years ago, I changed my life for this company. I did it because I recognized in it your passion. All my life I have wanted to be part of a company and a group of people who share a common vision. I saw that here in you, and I admire it.
>
> I'm here today because I love this company. I love what it represents . . . I know you're scared. I know you're concerned. Some of you may even be angry. But if you would just meet me halfway, I promise you I will not let you down. I promise you I will not leave anyone behind.[9]

Schultz had cast the vision. And in the coming months, he proved that he still valued great coffee. But he also went further. He began doing things that showed he valued the team. He called the people working for Starbucks "partners," and he backed it up with how he ran the company. He created a health plan that covered everyone, including part-timers. He clarified the company's mission and put into place a system in which hourly employees could hold management accountable to them. He even offered stock options to everyone, right down to the hourly employee who worked twenty hours a week making cappuccinos.

Schultz was trying to create the kind of company that people wanted to work for, the kind of place where someone like his father could have worked with dignity and respect. And he did it while making the company highly profitable. Starbucks is now a publicly traded company worth over $6 billion.[10] It serves more than 20 million people each week in more than 5,000 stores around the globe with plans to keep growing.[11] And it ranks high on the Forbes list of the best companies to work for.

Schultz sums up his role at Starbucks this way:

> I started off as a dreamer . . . Then I moved to entrepreneur . . . Then I had to become a manager, as the company grew larger and I needed to delegate more and more decisions. Today, my role is to be Starbucks' leader, its visionary, cheerleader, and keeper of the flame. [12]

Today Starbucks' customers, partners, and stockholders can clearly see the company's direction and have confidence in it. That's what vision does for a team. That's the power of the Law of the Compass.

Teamwork Thought

When you see it, you can seize it.

Becoming a Better Team Member

What is the vision for your team? You'd be surprised how many individuals are part of a group that works together but isn't clear about why. For example, that was the case when I became the leader of Skyline Church in the San Diego area. The church's board was comprised of twelve people. When I asked each member to articulate the church's vision the first time we met, I got eight different answers. A team can't move forward in confidence if it has no compass!

As a member of your team, you need a clear understanding of its vision. If the team doesn't have one, then help it to develop one. If the team has already found its compass and course, then you need to examine yourself in light of it to make sure there is a good match. If there isn't, you and your teammates are going to be frustrated. And everyone will probably be best served by a change.

Becoming a Better Team Leader

If you are the leader of your team, then you carry the responsibility for communicating the team's vision and keeping it before the people continually. That's not necessarily easy. Jack Welch, CEO of General Electric, observed, "Without question, communicating the vision, and the atmosphere around the vision, has been, and is continuing to be, by far, the toughest job we face."

I have found that people need to be shown the team's compass clearly, creatively, and continually. Whenever I endeavor to cast vision with the members of my team, I use the following checklist. I try to make sure that every vision message possesses . . .

- ❑ *Clarity:* brings understanding to the vision (answers what the people must know and what I want them to do)
- ❑ *Connectedness:* brings the past, present, and future together
- ❑ *Purpose:* brings direction to the vision
- ❑ *Goals:* bring targets to the vision

- ❑ *Honesty:* brings integrity to the vision and credibility to the vision caster
- ❑ *Stories:* bring relationships to the vision
- ❑ *Challenge:* brings stretching to the vision
- ❑ *Passion:* brings fuel to the vision
- ❑ *Modeling:* brings accountability to the vision
- ❑ *Strategy:* brings process to the vision

The next time you prepare to communicate vision to your people, use this checklist. Make sure you include each component, and I believe your team members will find the vision more accessible and will more readily buy into it. And if they do, you will see that they have greater direction and confidence.

8

THE LAW OF THE BAD APPLE

Rotten Attitudes Ruin a Team

Growing up, I loved basketball. It all started for me in the fourth grade when I saw a high school basketball game for the first time. I was captivated. Soon after that my dad poured a cement driveway along the side of our house and put a goal up on the garage for me. From that day until I went to college, I could usually be found practicing my shooting and playing pickup games on that small home court.

By the time I got to high school, I had become a pretty good player. I started on the junior varsity team as a freshman, and when I was a sophomore, our JV team had a 15-3 record, which was better than that of the varsity. We were proud of that—maybe a little too proud. I say that because of something that happened during my sophomore year.

One of the traditions on the team was that our coach, Don Neff, would give Ohio State basketball tickets to some of the players who had performed especially well during the season. Those players were almost always seniors, and they were always on the varsity. But that year I was one of the players offered Buckeye tickets. What was my response? Was I grateful and humbled by Coach Neff's recognition? No, I told him I thought he should let the JV play the varsity for *all* the tickets. Needless to say, he never allowed that game to be played.

The next year, critics who followed high school basketball in Ohio thought our team had a chance to win the state championship in our division. I guess they looked at the players who would return as seniors from the previous year's varsity team and saw the talent that would be moving up from the JV, and they figured we would be a powerhouse. And we did have a lot of talent. How many high school teams in the late 1960s could say that all but a couple of players on the team could dunk the ball? But the season turned out far different from everyone's expectations.

From Bad to Worse

From the beginning of the season, the team suffered problems. There were two of us juniors on the varsity who had the talent to start for the team: John Thomas, who was the team's best rebounder, and me, the best shooting guard. We thought playing time should be based strictly on ability, and we figured we deserved our place on the team. The seniors, who had taken a backseat to the previous year's seniors, thought we should be made to pay our dues and wait.

What began as a rivalry between the JV and varsity the year before turned into a war between the juniors and the seniors. When we scrimmaged at practice, it was the juniors against the seniors. In games the seniors wouldn't pass to the juniors and vice versa. We judged our success not by whether the team won or lost, but by whether the juniors' stats were better than those of the seniors. If we outshot, outpassed, and outrebounded the seniors, then we thought we had "won" the game, regardless of the outcome against our opponent.

The battles became so fierce that before long, the juniors and the seniors wouldn't even work together on the court during games. Coach Neff had to platoon us. The seniors would start, and when a substitution became necessary, he'd put not one but *five* juniors in the game. We became two teams on one roster.

I don't remember exactly who started the rivalry that split our team, but I do remember that John Thomas and I embraced it early on. I've always been a leader, and I did my share of influencing other team members. Unfortunately, I have to confess that I led the juniors in the wrong direction.

What started as a bad attitude in one or two players made a mess of the situation for everyone. By the time we were in the thick of our schedule, even the players who didn't want to take part in the rivalry were affected. The season was a disaster. In the end, we finished with a mediocre record and never came close to reaching our potential. It just goes to show you, *rotten attitudes ruin a team.* That's the Law of the Bad Apple.

Talent Is Not Enough

From my high school basketball experience I learned that talent is not enough to bring success to a team. Of course, you need talent. My friend Lou Holtz, the outstanding college football coach, observed, "You've got to have great athletes to win . . . You can't win without good athletes, but you can lose with them." But it also takes

> *Good attitudes among players do not guarantee a team's success, but bad attitudes guarantee its failure.*

much more than talented people to win.

My high school teammates were loaded with talent, and if that were enough, we could have been state champions. But we were also loaded with rotten attitudes. You know which won the battle between talent and attitude in the end. Perhaps that is why to this day I understand the importance of a positive attitude and have placed such a strong emphasis on it for myself, for my children as they were growing up, and for the teams I lead.

Years ago I wrote something about attitude for *The Winning Attitude.* I'd like to share it with you:

> Attitude . . .
> It is the "advance man" of our true selves.
> Its roots are inward but its fruit is outward.
> It is our best friend or our worst enemy.
> It is more honest and more consistent than our words.
> It is an outward look based on past experiences.
> It is a thing which draws people to us or repels them.
> It is never content until it is expressed.
> It is the librarian of our past.
> It is the speaker of our present.
> It is the prophet of our future.[1]

Good attitudes among players do not guarantee a team's success, but bad attitudes guarantee its failure.

The following five truths about attitudes clarify how they affect a team and teamwork.

1. Attitudes Have the Power to Lift Up or Tear Down a Team

In *The Winner's Edge* Denis Waitley stated, "The real leaders in business, in the professional community, in education, in government, and in the home also seem to draw upon a special cutting edge that separates them from the rest of society. The winner's edge is not in a gifted birth, in a high IQ, or in talent. The winner's edge is in the attitude, not aptitude."

Unfortunately, I think too many people resist that notion. They want to believe that talent alone (or talent with experience) is enough. But plenty of talented teams out there never amount to anything because of the attitudes of their players.

Various attitudes may impact a team made up of highly talented players:

Abilities	+	**Attitudes**	=	**Result**
Great Talent	+	Rotten Attitudes	=	Bad Team
Great Talent	+	Bad Attitudes	=	Average Team
Great Talent	+	Average Attitudes	=	Good Team
Great Talent	+	Good Attitudes	=	Great Team

If you want outstanding results, you need good people with great talent and awesome attitudes. When attitudes go up, so does the potential of the team. When attitudes go down, the potential of the team goes with it.

2. An Attitude Compounds When Exposed to Others

Several things on a team are not contagious. Talent. Experience. Willingness to practice. But you can be sure of one thing: Attitude is catching. When someone on the team is teachable and his humility is rewarded by improvement, others are more likely to display similar characteristics. When a leader is upbeat in the face of discouraging circumstances, others admire that quality and want to be like her. When a team member displays a strong work ethic and begins to have a positive impact, others imitate him. People become inspired by their peers. People have a tendency to adopt the attitudes of those they spend time with—to pick up on their mind-set, beliefs, and approaches to challenges.

The story of Roger Bannister is an inspiring example of the way attitudes often "compound." During the first half of the twentieth century, many sports experts believed that no runner could run a mile in less than four minutes. And for a long time they were right. But then on May 6, 1954, British runner and university student Roger Bannister ran a mile in 3 minutes 59.4 seconds during a meet in Oxford. Less than two months later, another runner, Australian John Landy, also broke the four-minute barrier. Then suddenly dozens and then hundreds of others broke it. Why? Because the best runners' attitudes changed. They began to adopt the mind-set and beliefs of their peers.

Bannister's attitude and actions compounded when exposed to others. His attitude spread. Today, every world-class runner who competes at that distance can run a mile in less than four minutes. Attitudes are contagious!

3. Bad Attitudes Compound Faster Than Good Ones

There's only one thing more contagious than a good attitude—and that's a bad attitude. For some reason many people think it's chic to be negative. I suspect that they think it makes them appear smart or important. But the truth is that a negative attitude hurts rather than helps the person who has it. And it also hurts the people around him.

A wise baseball manager once remarked that he never allowed the positive players to room with the negative ones on the road.

When he created the team's room assignments, he always put the negative ones together so that they couldn't poison anyone else.

To see how quickly and easily an attitude or mind-set can spread, just think about this story from Norman Cousins. Once during a football game, a doctor at the first aid station treated five people for what he suspected might be food poisoning. Since their symptoms were similar, he tried to track down what they had in common. He soon discovered that all five people had bought drinks from a particular concession stand at the stadium.

> *There's only one thing more contagious than a good attitude—and that's a bad attitude.*

The physician wanted to do the responsible thing, so he requested that the game's announcer advise people in the stadium to avoid buying drinks from the particular vendor because of the possibility of food poisoning. Before long, more than two hundred people complained of food poisoning symptoms. Nearly half the people's symptoms were so severe that they were taken to the hospital.

The story doesn't end there, however. After a little more detective work, it was discovered that the five original victims had eaten tainted potato salad from one particular deli on the way to the game. When the other "sufferers" found out that the drinks in the stadium were safe, they experienced miraculous recoveries. That just goes to show you, an attitude spreads very quickly.

4. Attitudes Are Subjective, So Identifying a Wrong One Can Be Difficult

Have you ever interacted with someone for the first time and suspected that his attitude was poor, yet you were unable to put your finger on exactly what was wrong? I believe many people have that experience.

The reason people doubt their observations about others' attitudes is that attitudes are subjective. Someone with a bad attitude may not do anything illegal or unethical. Yet his attitude may be ruining the team just the same.

People always project on the outside how they feel on the inside. Attitude is really about how a person is. That overflows into how he acts. Allow me to share with you common rotten attitudes that ruin a team so that you can recognize them for what they are when you see them.

An inability to admit wrongdoing. Have you ever spent time with people who *never* admit they're wrong? It's painful. Nobody's perfect, but someone who thinks he is does not make an ideal teammate. His wrong attitude will always create conflict.

Failing to forgive. It's said that Clara Barton, the founder of modern nursing, was once encouraged to bemoan a cruel act inflicted on her years earlier, but Barton wouldn't take the bait.

"Don't you remember the wrong that was done to you?" the friend goaded.

"No," answered Barton, "I distinctly remember forgetting that."

Holding a grudge is never positive or appropriate. And when unforgiveness occurs between teammates, it's certain to hurt the team.

Petty jealousy. An attitude that really works against people is the desire for equality that feeds petty jealousy. For some reason the people with this attitude believe that every person deserves equal treatment, regardless of talent, performance, or impact. Yet nothing could be farther from the truth. Each of us is created uniquely and performs differently, and as a result, we should be treated as such.

The disease of me. In his book *The Winner Within,* highly successful NBA coach Pat Riley writes about the "disease of me." He says of team members who have it, "They develop an overpowering belief in their own importance. Their actions virtually shout the claim,

'I'm the one.'" Riley asserts that the disease always has the same inevitable result: "The Defeat of Us."[2]

A critical spirit. Fred and Martha were driving home after a church service. "Fred," Martha asked, "did you notice that the pastor's sermon was kind of weak today?"

"No, not really," answered Fred.

"Well, did you hear that the choir was flat?"

"No, I didn't," he responded.

"Well, you certainly must have noticed that young couple and their children right in front of us, with all the noise and commotion they made the whole service!"

"I'm sorry, dear, but no, I didn't"

Finally in disgust Martha said, "Honestly, Fred, I don't know why you even bother to go to church."

When someone on the team has a critical spirit, everybody knows it because everyone on the team can do no right.

A desire to hog all the credit. Another bad attitude that hurts the team is similar to the "disease of me." But where the person with that disease may simmer in the background and create dissension, the credit hog continually steps into the spotlight to take a bow—whether he has earned it or not. His attitude is opposite that of NBA Hall of Fame center Bill Russell, who said of his time on the court, "The most important measure of how good a game I played was how much better I'd made my teammates play."

> *Most bad attitudes are the result of selfishness.*

Certainly there are other negative attitudes that I haven't named, but my intention isn't to list every bad attitude—just some of the most common ones. In a word, most bad attitudes are the result of selfishness. If one of your teammates puts others down, sabotages teamwork, or makes himself out to be more important than the team, then you can be sure that you've encountered someone with a bad attitude.

5. Rotten Attitudes, Left Alone, Ruin Everything

Bad attitudes must be addressed. You can be sure that they will always cause dissension, resentment, combativeness, and division on a team. And they will never go away on their own if they are left unaddressed. They will simply fester and ruin a team—along with its chances of reaching its potential.

Because people with bad attitudes are so difficult to deal with and because attitudes seem so subjective, you may doubt your gut reaction when you encounter a bad apple. After all, if it's only your *opinion* that he has a rotten attitude, then you have no right to address it, right? Not if you care about the team. *Rotten attitudes ruin a team.* That is always true. If you leave a bad apple in a barrel of good apples, you will always end up with a barrel of rotten apples.

President Thomas Jefferson remarked, "Nothing can stop the man with the right mental attitude from achieving his goal; nothing on earth can help the man with the wrong mental attitude." If you care about your team and you are committed to helping all of the players, you can't ignore a bad attitude. If you do, you will find out the hard way about the Law of the Bad Apple.

Your Best Friend or Worst Enemy

Attitude colors everything someone does. It determines how an individual sees the world and interacts with other people. A person's attitude—positively if it's good, negatively if it's not—always impacts his performance, regardless of talent, track record, or circumstances.

One of the most remarkable stories I've ever read that illustrates the Law of the Bad Apple came out of the San Francisco Bay area. Evidently the principal of a school called in three teachers to inform them of an experiment that the district would be conducting.

"Because you are the finest teachers in the system," she said, "we're going to give you ninety selected high-IQ students. We're going to let you move these students through this next year at their pace and see how much they can learn."

The faculty and students were delighted. During the next year, they had a wonderful experience. By the end of the last semester, the students had achieved 20 to 30 percent more than any other group of students in the area.

After the year was completed, the principal called in the teachers and told them, "I have a confession to make. I have to confess that you did not have ninety of the most intellectually prominent students. They were run-of-the-mill students. We took ninety students at random from the system and gave them to you."

The teachers were pleased. If the students were only average, that showed that the teachers had displayed exceptional skill and expertise.

"I have another confession," the principal continued. "You're not the brightest of the teachers. Your names were the first three names drawn out of a hat."

If the students and the teachers had been picked at random, then what had enabled them to make greater progress than any other group in the system? It was the attitudes of the people involved. Because the teachers and students expected to succeed, they increased their potential for success. Attitude had made all the difference.

If you want to give your team the best chance for success, then practice the Law of the Bad Apple. Trade your bad apples for good ones and you have a chance, because *rotten apples ruin a team.*

Teamwork Thought

Your attitude determines the team's attitude.

Becoming a Better Team Member

The first place to start when it comes to attitude is yourself. How are you doing? For example, do you . . .

- ❑ Think the team wouldn't be able to get along without you?
- ❑ Secretly (or not so secretly) believe that recent team successes are really attributable to your personal efforts, not the work of the whole team?
- ❑ Keep score when it comes to the praise and perks handed out to other team members?
- ❑ Have a hard time admitting when you make a mistake? (If you believe you're not making mistakes, you need to check this!)
- ❑ Bring up past wrongs from your teammates?
- ❑ Believe that you are being grossly underpaid?

If you could place a check next to any of them, then you need to check your attitude.

Talk to your teammates, and find out if your attitude is doing damage to the team. Talk to your leader. And if you really think your pay is inequitable, you need to talk it out with your employer and find out where you stand. Anytime a relationship is unequal, it cannot last—whether you are giving more than you get or getting more than you deserve. In either case, the relationship will break down.

Warning! I have one word of caution: If you leave your position because you believe you are undervalued, and you don't succeed in your new situation, then you most likely overestimated your value or underestimated what the organization was doing to help you succeed.

Becoming a Better Team Leader

If you think you have a bad apple on your team, you need to take the person aside and discuss the situation with him. Doing it the right way is important. Take the high road: As you approach him, share what you have observed, but give him the benefit of the doubt. Assume that your perception might be wrong and you want clarification. (If you have several people with bad attitudes, start with the ringleader.) If it truly is your perception and the team is not being hurt, then you haven't done any damage, and you have smoothed the relationship between you and the other person.

However, if it turns out that your perception was correct and the person's attitude is the problem, give him clear expectations and an opportunity to change. Then hold him accountable. If he changes, it's a win for the team. If he doesn't, remove him from the team. You cannot allow him to remain because you can be sure his *rotten attitude will ruin the team.*

COMPANION ONLINE RESOURCE

Learn more about how the Law of the Bad Apple uniquely applies to you.

Take the FREE Law of the Bad Apple assessment at **LawsOfTeamwork.com**.

9

THE LAW OF COUNTABILITY

Teammates Must Be Able to Count on Each Other When It Counts

One of the many strong points of Atlanta, Georgia, where I moved my family and my companies in 1997, is that it's a sports town. I don't get the chance to go to a lot of games, but there are few things I like better than attending a sporting event with all of the energy and excitement. Watching a team with a friend or two is a joy, whether it's the Braves (baseball), the Hawks (basketball), the Falcons (football), or the Thrashers (hockey).

When the announcement was made that Atlanta would be getting a hockey team, plans were set in motion to build the team a new arena. The old Omni, where the Hawks had played since the early 1970s, was slated to be demolished and replaced on the same site by the Philips Arena. It would be an 18,000-seat state-of-the-art entertainment complex with box seating, which could host not only hockey and basketball but also concerts and other events.

Tearing down the Omni wasn't going to be a routine process. First, it needed to be done quickly so that construction could begin on the new arena. Second, because the old structure had a cantilevered roof, taking the building apart in opposite order from the way it was constructed was out of the question. It would be far too dangerous for the demolition crews. That left only one choice: blowing it up.

Explosive Family Business

When demolition crews need help blowing up a building—or more accurately imploding a building—they inevitably turn to the Loizeaux family, the people who pioneered the safe demolition of buildings using explosives. They are owners and founders of Controlled Demolition Incorporated (CDI). The company was founded by Jack Loizeaux who had started a company in the 1940s removing tree stumps with dynamite. In 1957, he blasted his first building. And in the 1960s, he began CDI. Since that first demolition—an apartment building in Washington, D.C., his company has demolished more than seven thousand structures worldwide.

CDI is a family operation. Jack and his wife, Freddie, ran the business in the beginning. It wasn't long before they were joined by their sons, Mark and Doug. When Jack retired in 1976, his sons took over the operation. Today, they are joined by several of Mark's children, including his daughter Stacey, in her early thirties, who has worked in the field since age fifteen and is already an expert in her own right.

Like Threading a Needle

When the Loizeauxs were contacted for the job, they quickly discovered that the demolition wouldn't be easy because of the Omni's proximity to other buildings. On one side was the World Congress Center, which is used for conventions. On another side was a station for MARTA (Atlanta's mass-transit rail system). On the third was the CNN Center from which cable and radio programming broadcasts twenty-four hours a day. And CNN Plaza was a mere thirteen feet away from the Omni! A mistake could damage the MARTA line and shut it down at one of its busiest stations. Or it could put CNN news service temporarily out of business. And of course in a worst-case scenario, the Omni could topple in the wrong direction and take down the CNN building itself. It would take every bit of the Loizeauxs' expertise and fifty years of experience to do the task right.

Using explosives to take down a building is always a dangerous undertaking. Each project is different and requires a custom-made strategy. Holes are drilled in strategic places in many parts of the structure, such as in columns, and filled with appropriate amounts of explosive material. Then those blast points are often wrapped in chain-link fence (to catch the big pieces upon detonation) and wrapped in a special fabric that helps contain the explosion. "It allows the concrete to move, but it keeps the concrete from flying," says Stacey Loizeaux. "We also sometimes put up a curtain around the entire floor, to catch stuff that gets through these first two layers. That's really where your liability is."[1] Often, earthen berms are also erected around the building to protect nearby people and structures.

Obviously there is risk anytime someone works with explosives. But the greatest danger comes in the way explosives are rigged to go off. To get the building to fall in on itself, the Loizeauxs and their crew have to precisely sequence the charges, often using delays that differ from one another by the tiniest fractions of a second. That was the case for the Omni, where first the roof needed to fall straight down, then three of the walls would need to fall inward, and then the fourth wall outward. And on July 26, 1997, at 6:53 A.M., that's exactly the way it happened. The demolition took ten seconds.

When it comes to blowing up a building the way the Loizeauxs do, everything has to go right—from analyzing the building, to planning the demolition, to transporting the explosives, to rigging the devices, to preparing the building for the safety of the surrounding area. If anyone on the crew fails to get his part right and lets the other members of the team down, not only does the CDI team fail in its objective, but it also puts a lot of people and property in danger. *Teammates must be able to count on each other when it counts.* That's the Law of Countability.

Holding Each Other Accountable

The importance of the Law of Countability is clearest when the stakes are high. But you don't have to be in an explosive situation for the law to come into play. The person running a business who is trying to get out a product on schedule depends on her vendors to deliver on their promises during crunch time. The waiter trying to please his customer counts on the kitchen staff to prepare the food properly. The mom getting ready for a job interview has to know that her baby-sitter will show up as promised. If there is a breakdown in countability, then the account is lost, the customer goes away unhappy, and the job goes to some other candidate. *Teammates must be able to count on each other when it counts.*

I was reminded of how often we encounter examples of the Law of Countability, even in small things, when I was on a trip to South Africa. I was there to teach at a conference sponsored by EQUIP, my nonprofit organization. I was waiting in the hotel lobby for my ride to the conference, and I was having some trouble with a cough. That's usually no big deal, but when you're preparing to speak for five or six hours straight, it's not a great way to start the day. As the conference team and I got under way, Erick Moon, a member of the team, pulled a Ricola cough drop (my brand) out of his pocket and handed it to me. When he saw my surprise, he said simply, "We're all carrying them for you, just in case."

> *"We don't work for each other; we work with each other."*
>
> —STANLEY C. GAULT

Stanley C. Gault asserted, "We don't work for each other; we work with each other." That is the essence of countability—it's the ability and desire for teammates to work together toward common goals. But that doesn't happen on its own. Nor is countability a given. It has to be earned. Team members who can depend on each other only during the easy times have not developed countability.

The Formula for Countability

I believe that there is a formula for countability. It's not complicated, but its impact is powerful. Here it is:

Character + Competence + Commitment +
Consistency + Cohesion =
Countability

When every team member embraces each of these five qualities, within himself and with others, the team can achieve the countability that is necessary to succeed.

1. Character

In *The 21 Irrefutable Laws of Leadership,* I wrote about the Law of Solid Ground, which says that trust is the foundation of leadership. That law is really about character. In the book I state, "Character makes trust possible. Trust makes leadership possible. That is the Law of Solid Ground."[2]

> *"There is no substitute for character. You can buy brains, but you cannot buy character."*
>
> —ROBERT A. COOK

In a similar way, countability begins with character because it is based on trust, which is the foundation for all interaction with people. If you cannot trust someone, you will not count on him. As Robert A. Cook remarked, "There is no substitute for character. You can buy brains, but you cannot buy character."

Anytime you desire to build a team, you have to begin by building character in the individuals who make up the team. For example, my friend Lou Holtz, who coaches football at the University of South Carolina, introduces the players on his team to a list of twelve covenants at the beginning of the season to help them understand the team culture he is trying to create. Here are the covenants:

USC—12 Covenants

1. We will accomplish what we do together. We share our success, and we never let any one of us fail alone.

2. We are all fully grown adults. We will act as such, and expect the same from the people around us.

3. We will not keep secrets. Information that affects us all will be shared by all of us, and we will quickly and openly work to separate fact from fiction.

4. We will not lie to ourselves or to each other. None of us will tolerate any of us doing so. We will depend on each other for the truth.

5. We will keep our word. We will say what we mean, and do what we say. We trust the word of others to be good as well.

6. We will keep our head. We will not panic in the face of tough times. We will always choose to roll up our sleeves rather than wring our hands.

7. We will develop our abilities and take pride in them. We will set our own standards higher than our most challenging opponent, and we will please our fans by pleasing ourselves.

8. We will treat our locker room like home and our teammates like friends. We spend too much time together to allow these things to go bad.

9. We will be unselfish and expect that everyone else will exhibit this same quality. We will care about each other without expectations.

10. We will look out for each other. We truly believe that we are our brother's keeper.

11. We are students at USC, and as such we will strive to graduate. We take pride in our grade point average and expect our teammates to do the same.

12. Losing cannot and will not be tolerated in anything we do. Losing to us is to be shamed, embarrassed, and humiliated. There is no excuse for losing a football game at USC.

When you read through the twelve points, did you notice anything? Most of them touch on issues of character. Holtz knows that if he doesn't lay a solid foundation of character within the young men on his team, he can't build anything of value on top of it.

Barry Gibbons, in his book *This Indecision Is Final,* asserted, "Write and publish what you want, but the only missions, values, and ethics that count in your company are those that manifest themselves in the behavior of all the people, all the time."[3]

> *"Write and publish what you want, but the only missions, values, and ethics that count in your company are those that manifest themselves in the behavior of all the people, all the time."*
>
> —BARRY GIBBONS

2. Competence

I spent over twenty-five years as a pastor, so I know the church world very well, and I have seen people in the religious community who act as if character is the only thing that matters. I don't think that's true. What you do is also important, as Scripture makes clear.[4] Character is the most important thing, but it's not the only thing.

If you have any doubts about that, consider this. If you had to go into surgery because of a life-threatening illness, would you be happier having a good surgeon who was a bad person or a good person who was a bad surgeon? That puts it in perspective, doesn't it? Competence matters. And if the person is going to be on the same team with you, you want competence *and* character.

3. Commitment

Having fair-weather team members doesn't make for a very pleasant team experience. When times are tough, you want to know that you can count on your teammates. You don't want to be wondering whether they're going to hang in there with you.

Dan Reiland, who is a vice president at The INJOY Group, shared with me the table on the next page that indicates the commitment of various team members.

Teams succeed or fail based on teammates' commitment to one another and the team. My friend Randy Watts, who pastors a church in Virginia, sent me a note after a conference where I taught the Law of Countability. He wrote:

> Years ago, a friend of mine attended the Virginia Military Institute, known for its rugged physical, mental, and emotional training. He told me that all the incoming freshmen are separated into companies. One of their training obstacles is to race up House Mountain, which is very steep and more than a challenge. The motivation for climbing: If you finish last, you run again. Not you, but your whole company! This makes for team commitment. If a person in your company twists an ankle or breaks a leg, other members of his company carry him! It is not enough to be the first man on top of the mountain; everyone on the team has to make it.

Real teamwork requires that kind of commitment. When teammates can't make it, you carry them the rest of the way for the sake of the team.

Level	Type of Teammate	Description
1. Green Beret Colonel	Committed Team Leader	*Dedicated to the cause. Focused on the big picture. Has a whatever-it-takes attitude.*
2. First Lieutenant	Team Achiever	*Buys into the spirit and culture of the organization. Is self-motivated and productive.*
3. OCS Graduates	Genuine Team Player	*Has passion and enthusiasm. Arrives early and stays late. Is not yet a proven leader.*
4. Private	Formal Team Member	*Enjoys being on the team. Wants to stay. Serves out of duty. Not yet a high achiever.*
5. Boot Camp Recruit	Begrudging Follower	*Will work, but only with a kick in the seat of the pants.*
6. Deserter	Nonfollower	*Won't do anything. Needs to be court-martialed.*
7. Sniper	Dangerous Follower	*Works, but makes life difficult for team. Will shoot teammates if given the chance.*

4. Consistency

Every once in a while somebody comes along who defines consistency for the rest of his teammates. In the case of the Atlanta Braves, I believe that person is Greg Maddux. If you follow baseball, then you probably know about him. Maddux is a first-rate pitcher, and he has the awards—and statistics—to prove it. He has won more than 200 games, including 176 games in the 1990s, the most of any pitcher in major-league baseball. He is the only pitcher besides Cy Young and Gaylord Perry to have won 15 or more games in 13 consecutive seasons. He is the only pitcher in baseball's history to have won the Cy Young Award four years in a row (1992–95).

For all of Maddux's awards for pitching and noteworthy stats, do you know what has been his most remarkable honor? He has been recognized as the National League's best fielder in his position by receiving a Gold Glove *ten years in a row!*

Many great pitchers are not known for their fielding. When a difficult ball is hit to a pitcher, or when the pitcher has to cover first base on a tough play to the right side of the infield, many times the other players on the team hold their collective breath. If anyone on the field is likely to make a fielding mistake, it's the pitcher. But not Maddux. He works at his fielding with the same fantastic work ethic that has made him an outstanding pitcher. The result is a career that has seen only fourteen errors in fifteen years (with two seasons of error-free fielding).

If you want your teammates to have confidence in you, to know they can count on you day in and day out, then use someone like Maddux as your example. Consistency is key.

5. Cohesion

Teammates need to develop cohesion. That's the ability to hold together, no matter how difficult the circumstances become. Navy SEAL John Roat describes cohesion this way:

> Unit cohesion is one of those terms that everyone thinks they understand. In truth, most people don't have a clue. It is definitely

> not about everybody liking each other or being nice. It means you have a pride in the ability of your group to function at a higher level than possible for the individual. The unit doesn't shine because you're a member, you shine because you're good enough to be a member.[5]

There's an old saying when it comes to teams: Either we're pulling together or we're pulling apart. Without cohesion people aren't really a team because they're not pulling together. They're merely a group of individuals working for the same organization.

> *There's an old saying when it comes to teams: Either we're pulling together or we're pulling apart.*

Novelist and civil rights activist James Baldwin asserted, "The moment we break faith with one another, the sea engulfs us and the light goes out." When it comes down to it, countability is being able to have faith in your teammates, no matter what happens. When the chips are down, you can turn to the people on your team. Let's face it: You can't do anything that counts unless you have countability. *Teammates must be able to count on each other when it really counts.*

Broken Trust

When you see a major example of broken trust that destroys countability on a team, you know it instantly. When parents run out on their children, a spouse is guilty of infidelity, or children callously deceive their parents, it is a violation of countability in the family. When employees embezzle money, or leaders abuse the power entrusted to them by people in their organization, it undermines countability in a business. And when an officer in a government agency is guilty of espionage, it not only hurts his teammates; it breaks trust with the people in an entire nation.

When the news broke in early 2001 that an FBI agent had been caught passing highly classified national security information to Russia and the former Soviet Union, the first thing I thought of was the Law of Countability. The man in this case was Robert Philip Hanssen, a counterintelligence agent who had made a career with the FBI.

Hanssen is suspected of having given the KGB (and the organization that replaced it called the SVR) sensitive information on more than twenty occasions. That information totaled more than six thousand pages of material, including counterintelligence investigative techniques, sources, methods, and operations.[6] And just as in the case of Aldridge Ames, the CIA counterintelligence officer convicted of espionage in 1994, the information illegally passed by Hanssen is believed to have precipitated the deaths of field agents working for the U.S. government.[7]

Nobody likes a traitor. In fact, in America, the name Benedict Arnold is still associated with treachery and betrayal, even though his actions occurred more than two hundred years ago. (And few remember that Arnold was a brilliant military leader.) But what makes Hanssen's case especially distasteful is that the betrayer was a member of a team that maintains high standards of conduct because of the trust given to it by the people. The FBI identifies its core values as "rigorous obedience to the Constitution of the United States; respect for the dignity of all those we protect; compassion; fairness; and uncompromising personal and institutional integrity."[8] FBI Director Louis J. Freeh said of Hanssen:

> A betrayal of trust by an FBI agent, who is not only sworn to enforce the law but specifically to help protect our nation's security, is particularly abhorrent. This kind of criminal conduct represents the most traitorous action imaginable . . . It also strikes at the heart of everything the FBI represents—the commitment of over 28,000 honest and dedicated men and women in the FBI who work diligently to earn the trust and confidence of the American people every day.[9]

In other words, *teammates must be able to count on each other when it counts.* Robert Hanssen broke the trust that makes countability possible. And it may be decades before we find out how much damage he did to the country. That's a terrible thought, but that's the price that sometimes has to be paid when someone breaks the Law of Countability.

Teamwork Thought

The greatest compliment you can receive is being counted on.

Becoming a Better Team Member

People often say that imitation is a compliment. In regard to teamwork I believe the highest compliment you can receive is trust from your teammates when it really counts.

How do your teammates feel about you? In Chapter 6 we talked about how catalysts step up to a higher level of play when crunch time comes. You may or may not be the type of player who can make things happen and then some when the game is on the line. That's okay. But can you be depended on to do *your* part, whatever that is, when your teammates need you? Do you perform and follow through in such a way that the team considers you someone they can count on? How are you doing in each of the areas examined in the chapter?

- Is your integrity unquestioned (character)?
- Do you perform your work with excellence (competence)?
- Are you dedicated to the team's success (commitment)?
- Can you be depended on every time (consistency)?
- Do your actions bring the team together (cohesion)?

If you are weak in any of these areas, talk to a mentor or trusted friend to get suggestions concerning how you can grow in that area.

Becoming a Better Team Leader

Developing countability and cohesion among team members is not always an easy task. And it takes time. If you are responsible for leading your team, use the suggestions of William A. Cohen in *The Art of the Leader* for building a team that is able to count on each member when it counts:

1. Develop pride in group membership.
2. Convince your group that they are the best.
3. Give recognition whenever possible.

4. Encourage organizational mottos, names, symbols, and slogans.
5. Establish your group's worth by examining and promoting its history and values.
6. Focus on the common purpose.
7. Encourage your people to participate in activities together outside of work.[10]

The more of these activities you embrace, the greater countability you will develop.

COMPANION ONLINE RESOURCE

Learn more about how the Law of Countability uniquely applies to you.

Take the FREE Law of Countability assessment at **LawsOfTeamwork.com**.

10

THE LAW OF THE PRICE TAG

The Team Fails to Reach Its Potential When It Fails to Pay the Price

On December 28, 2000, one of the nation's oldest retailers, Montgomery Ward and Company, announced that it would be filing Chapter 7 bankruptcy and closing its doors forever. That announcement saddened the people of Chicago, for Ward had been an institution in that city for more than a century. What's even sadder is that the company's failure might have been avoided if leaders had learned and practiced the Law of the Price Tag before it was too late.

The retailing chain's early history is really quite remarkable. The company was founded in 1872 by Aaron Montgomery Ward, a young salesman who had worked for various dry goods merchants throughout the Midwest and South. While he was working in rural areas far from cities or large towns, he discovered that many consumers in remote areas were at the mercy of local merchants who often overcharged them for merchandise. That gave him an idea. Railroads and mail service were improving by that time. What if he bought dry goods directly from manufacturers for cash and sold them for cash via mail order to rural consumers, thus eliminating the middlemen who were gouging those customers?

Paying the First Price

In 1871, Ward saved enough money from his work as a salesman to purchase some merchandise and print a one-page price list that he planned to mail out to a bunch of farmers who belonged to a fraternal organization. But before he could follow through with his plan, the devastating Chicago fire of 1871 destroyed his stock and price sheets. The setback didn't stop Ward. He convinced two sales colleagues to join him as partners, began rebuilding his stock, and reprinted the price sheet, which would become the world's first general merchandise mail-order catalog. And in 1872, at age twenty-eight, Ward opened for business.

At first, Ward was only moderately successful. In fact, a year into the business, his two partners got cold feet and asked to be bought out. Ward paid them off, then took his friend George Thorne into the business as a full partner. Together they worked hard, taking orders and shipping out merchandise by rail. Meanwhile, in 1875, Ward and Thorne came up with a novel idea. They decided to include a new credo in their catalog. It said, "Satisfaction Guaranteed or Your Money Back." And the business took off.

Ward's tenacity and willingness to pay the price twice for starting his own business came to fruition less than a decade later. The company that had begun with $1,600 of capital in 1872 had sales of

$300,000 in 1878. Nine years after that, the company's sales rose to $1 million. By the turn of the century, Montgomery Ward and Company's catalog, which would come to be known as the "Wish Book," grew to five hundred pages and was being mailed to more than a million people every year. And the company's headquarters was a new building on Michigan Avenue in Chicago—the biggest skyscraper west of New York City.[1]

Stopping Payment

Then in 1901, Montgomery Ward retired in order to spend the final years of his life working to make Chicago a better place. During the first two decades of the new century, the company continued to thrive. But in the late 1910s, things began to change. Ward's success had prompted the start of another Chicago-based company in 1886: Sears, Roebuck, and Co. It, like Montgomery Ward and Company, was a catalog-based merchant that catered to rural customers. Back when both companies began business, most of the U.S. population lived in rural areas. But the country was changing. Cities were filling up. When the 1920 census was completed, it showed that for the first time in the nation's history, the majority of the population lived in urban centers—and shopping habits were changing as a result.

Robert E. Wood, a former army quartermaster general, was brought in to run Montgomery Ward in 1919, and he saw the coming boom in retail sales. He wanted to begin opening stores in cities where people could shop in person, but the owners were unwilling to go along with the idea.[2] They simply would not pay the price to make the change.

Passed By

Knowing where the future lay in the business, Wood left Ward. In 1924, he went on staff at Sears as vice president. He convinced the people who ran Sears to take a chance on retail store sales. They agreed to open one store in Chicago as a test the following year. It was an immediate success. Two years later, Sears had opened 27 stores. By 1929, the company had built more than 300. Even during the depression, Sears continued to expand, and in 1931, Sears retail store sales surpassed catalog sales.[3] Wood became the company's chairman, a position he held until 1954, and Sears became the most successful department store chain in the country.

Montgomery Ward and Company never really recovered from that early error. It opened some retail stores, but it wasn't aggressive enough to overtake Sears. *The team fails to reach its potential when it fails to pay the price.* Time after time, Ward failed to pay the price. During the depression, the company hoarded cash and stopped expansion while Sears gained more ground. After World War II when other stores began moving to the suburbs, Ward failed to seize the opportunity to try to get back on top. Each time the market changed, the company's leaders didn't pay the price necessary to win a market. For the last twenty-five years of the twentieth century, they struggled to keep their doors open. Finally, after 128 years in business, Montgomery Ward closed. That's what can happen when people violate the Law of the Price Tag.

Price Points

If a team doesn't reach its potential, seldom is ability the issue. It's rarely a matter of resources either. It's almost always a payment issue. Montgomery Ward and Company had plenty of resources, and it had the talent it needed, including the leader who could move the team forward. The problem was that the company's owners were unwilling to get out of their comfort zone, take a risk, and try to break new ground.

One of the reasons teams fail to pay the price to reach their potential is that they misunderstand the Law of the Price Tag. They honestly don't know how it works. Allow me to give you four truths about this law that will help to clarify it in your mind.

1. The Price Must Be Paid by Everyone

In *Straight Talk for Monday Morning*, Allan Cox observed:

> You have to give up something to be a member of a team. It may be a phony role you've assigned to yourself, such as the guy who talks too much, the woman who remains silent, the know-it-all, the know-nothing, the hoarder of talented subordinates, the non-sharer of some resource such as management information systems (MIS), or whatever. You give up something, to be sure, such as some petty corner of privilege, but gain authenticity in return. The team, moreover, doesn't quash individual accomplishment; rather it empowers personal contributions.[4]

> *If everyone doesn't pay the price to win, then everyone will pay the price by losing.*

People who've never had the experience of being on a winning team often fail to realize that *every* team member must pay a price. I think some of them think that if others work hard, they can coast to their potential. But that is never true. If everyone doesn't pay the price to win, then everyone will pay the price by losing.

2. The Price Must Be Paid All the Time

Many people have what I call destination disease. I describe it in my book *The 21 Indispensable Qualities of a Leader*:

> Some people mistakenly believe that if they can accomplish a particular goal, they no longer have to grow. It can happen with almost anything: earning a degree, reaching a desired position, receiving a particular award, or achieving a financial goal.
>
> But effective leaders cannot afford to think that way. The day they stop growing is the day they forfeit their potential—and the potential of their organization. Remember the words of Ray Kroc: "As long as you're green, you're growing. As soon as you're ripe, you start to rot."[5]

Destination disease is as dangerous for a team as it is for any individual. It makes us believe that we can stop working, stop striving, stop paying the price—yet still reach our potential. But as Earl Blaik, former football coach at the United States Military Academy, observed, "There is no substitute for work. It is the price of success." That truth never goes away. That's why President Dwight D. Eisenhower remarked, "There are no victories at bargain prices." If you want to reach your potential, you can never let up.

> *"There are no victories at bargain prices."*
>
> —DWIGHT D. EISENHOWER

3. The Price Increases If the Team Wants to Improve, Change, or Keep Winning

As I mentioned in the introduction of this book, there are few back-to-back champions in sports. And few companies stay at the top of *Forbes* magazine's lists for a decade. Becoming a champion has a high price. But remaining on top costs even more. And improving upon your best is even more costly. The higher you are, the more you have to pay to make even small improvements. World champion sprinters improve their times not by seconds, but by hundredths of a second.

No one can move closer to his potential without paying in some way to get there. If you want to change professions, you have to get more education, additional work experience, or both. If you want to run a race at a faster pace, you must pay by training harder and smarter. If you want to increase earnings from your investments, you put in more money or take greater risks. The same principle applies to teams. To improve, change, or keep winning, as a group the team must pay a price, and so must the individuals on it.

4. The Price Never Decreases

Most people who quit don't give up at the bottom of the mountain; they stop halfway up it. Nobody sets out with the purpose of losing. The problem is often a mistaken belief that a time will come when success will suddenly get cheaper. But life rarely works that way.

> *Most people who quit don't give up at the bottom of the mountain; they stop halfway up it.*

Maybe that kind of thinking was the problem with Montgomery Ward and Company. In 1919, when the decision makers had the chance to make Ward one of the first big companies to open a chain of retail stores, they probably evaluated what it would cost them—in terms of time, money, effort, change—and they thought that it was too great a price to pay. So they passed on the opportunity.

A few years later when Sears began to breeze past Ward, the cost to compete was even higher. The company paid to get into retail store sales, yet it was still behind. That price continued to go up year after year, especially as Sears beat Ward in securing prime locations. Even as late as the 1970s and 1980s, Ward paid more and more to improve, yet fell farther and farther behind. The company dabbled in various niches, trying to compete against Wal-Mart, Target, and Circuit City, but it kept getting clobbered. The leaders thought the price would be less the next time—but it kept going up and up.

> *When it comes to the Law of the Price Tag, I believe there are really only two kinds of teams who violate it: those who don't realize the price of success, and those who know the price but are not willing to pay it.*

When it comes to the Law of the Price Tag, I believe there are really only two kinds of teams who violate it: those who don't realize the price of success, and those who know the price but are not willing to pay it. No one can force a team member to have the will to succeed. Each person must decide in his own heart whether the goal is worth the price that must be paid. But every person ought to know what to expect to pay in order for a team to succeed.

The Price of Teamwork

For that reason, I offer the following observations about the cost of being part of a winning team. To become team players, you and your teammates will have at least the following required of you:

Sacrifice

There can be no success without sacrifice. James Allen observed, "He who would accomplish little must sacrifice little; he who would achieve much must sacrifice much." When you become part of a team, you may be aware of some of the things you will have to give up. But you can be sure that no matter how much you expect to give for the team, at some point you will be required to give more. That's the nature of teamwork. The team gets to the top only through the sweat, blood, and sacrifice of its team members.

Time Commitment

Teamwork does not come cheaply. It costs you time—that means you pay for it with your life. It takes time to get to know people, to build relationships with them, to learn how you and they work together. Teamwork can't be developed in microwave time. Teams grow strong in a Crock-Pot environment.

Personal Development

Your team will reach its potential only if you reach your potential. That means today's ability is not enough. Or to put it the way leadership expert Max DePree did: "We cannot become what we need to be by remaining what we are." That desire to keep striving,

Your team will reach its potential only if you reach your potential.

to keep getting better, is a key to your ability, but it is also crucial for the betterment of the team. That is why UCLA's John Wooden, a marvelous team leader and the greatest college basketball coach of all time, said, "It's what you learn after you know it all that counts."

Unselfishness

People naturally look out for themselves. The question "What's in it for me?" is never far from their thoughts. But if a team is to reach its potential, its players must put the team's agenda ahead of their own. Some people see the big picture more easily than others do and realize that they will receive more if they give more. For others, that is more difficult—especially if they already have a track record of high achievement. But H. Jackson Brown's Boomerang Theory is true: "When you give your best to the world, the world returns the favor." And if you give your best to the team, it will return more to you than you give, and together you will achieve more than you can on your own.

"When you give your best to the world, the world returns the favor."

—H. JACKSON BROWN

Certainly there are other prices individuals must pay to be part of a team. You can probably list several specific ones you've paid to be on a team. The point is that people can choose to stand on the sidelines of life and try to do everything solo. Or they can get into the game by being part of a team. It's a trade-off between independence and interdependence. The rewards of teamwork can be great, but there is always a cost. You always have to give up to go up.

About a month ago I was teaching the 17 Laws of Teamwork to a group of businesspeople in Atlanta, and after I taught the Law of the Price Tag, Virgil Berry came up to me and slipped me a note. It said, "John, the price tag for failure is greater than the price of success. The price for accepting failure is poverty, depression, dejection, and a downtrodden spirit." The people at Montgomery Ward know that all too well. *The team fails to reach its potential when it fails to pay the price.*

What Price for a Nation?

Paying a high price does not always guarantee victory. Many teams sacrifice dearly, only to fall short of their goals. But sometimes great sacrifice is rewarded with great results. That was the case for the Revolutionary Army of the newly formed United States and its commander, George Washington, during the winter of 1777 in Valley Forge, Pennsylvania.

The year 1777 was not a particularly successful one for General Washington and his troops. Following defeats at Brandywine, Paoli, and Germantown and the loss of Philadelphia to the British, Washington and eleven thousand soldiers straggled into Valley Forge on December 19 of that year. The troops were demoralized, and they were facing the prospect of a bitter winter with minimal shelter and comforts.

What those men probably wanted most was to go home and forget about the war for freedom. But if they did, the cost would be high. Positioned as they were, they could keep an eye on the British troops under General Howe in Philadelphia. More important, they were in a place where they could defend York, Pennsylvania, to which the Continental Congress had fled when the capital fell to the British. If the men at Valley Forge didn't pay the price, the government would fall, the army would be disbanded, and the Revolutionary War would be lost.

Conditions were horrible. The men were ill-equipped and poorly supplied. A few days after their arrival, Washington wrote to the Continental Congress, saying, "2,898 men were unfit for duty because they were barefoot or otherwise naked [insufficiently clothed for the harsh weather]." Things were so bad that sentries had to stand on their hats to ward off frostbite in their feet. By February 1, 1778, only 5,000 men were available for service.[6]

Paying the Price—and Then Some

Miraculously, the troops didn't give up. They bore the brunt of the difficult winter. But they did more than just hang on and survive. They took the time to become better soldiers. Prior to their stay at Valley Forge, they were disorganized and untrained. To remedy that, General Washington employed the talents of a former officer in the Prussian army, Baron von Steuben.

First, von Steuben imposed organization on the camp and introduced improved sanitation. Then, under his instruction, one company of men was transformed into a crack team of soldiers. They in turn helped to train the other companies of men. Von Steuben also standardized the military maneuvers throughout the army so that the men could work better as a team, no matter which officers commanded them. By the time the army mobilized in June of 1778, it was a match for any group of soldiers, even the British, who were considered by some to be the best in the world.

Washington's army went on to win battles against a British army with far superior numbers. And his soldiers fought in the Battle of Yorktown, the decisive battle that turned the war in favor of the newly formed country. Those of us who live in the United States are grateful to them, for the price they paid more than two hundred years ago paved the way for us to live in a country of great freedom and opportunity. While it's true that *the team fails to reach its potential when it fails to pay the price,* it's also true that when the price *is* paid, the rewards can be abundant. That's the blessing of the Law of the Price Tag.

Teamwork Thought

You seldom get more than you pay for.

Becoming a Better Team Member

If you are an achiever, then you probably have lots of dreams and goals. Write down some of the things you desire to accomplish in the next one to five years:

1. ______________________________

2. ______________________________

3. ______________________________

4. ______________________________

5. ______________________________

6. ______________________________

7. ______________________________

8. ______________________________

9. ______________________________

10. ______________________________

Now, which of them are you willing to give up? You always need to be ready to ask yourself that question when you are part of a team. When your personal goals conflict with the greater goals of your team, you have three choices:

1. Put down the goal (because the team is more important).

2. Put off the goal (because it's not the right time).

3. Part with the team (because it's better for everyone).

The one thing you have no right to do is to expect the team to sacrifice its collective goals for yours.

Becoming a Better Team Leader

If you lead a team, then you must convince your teammates to sacrifice for the good of the group. The more talented the team members, the more difficult it may be to convince them to put the team first.

Begin by modeling sacrifice. Show the team that you are . . .

- Willing to make financial sacrifices for the team.
- Willing to keep growing for the sake of the team.
- Willing to empower others for the sake of the team.
- Willing to make difficult decisions for the sake of the team.

Once you have modeled the willingness to pay a price for the potential of the team, you have the credibility to ask others to do the same. Then when you recognize sacrifices that teammates must make for the team, show them why and how to do it. Then praise their sacrifices to their teammates.

11

THE LAW OF THE SCOREBOARD

The Team Can Make Adjustments When It Knows Where It Stands

In the previous chapter, you read about Montgomery Ward and Company, an American business that fell on hard times because it failed to heed the Law of the Price Tag. For a couple of decades, it looked as if another American institution was headed for a similar disaster: Walt Disney Productions.

The Mouse That Roared

The company was founded by Walt Disney and his brother, Roy, in the 1920s. They began doing silent animation shorts and grew the company into one of the most loved and respected entertainment companies in the world. They continually broke new ground. They produced the first talking cartoon and the first color cartoon, both featuring Mickey Mouse, who has since become an American icon. *Snow White,* the first feature-length animated movie ever, was a radically innovative idea. While it was being made, many called it "Disney's folly." When it was released in 1937, it became the most successful film ever made up to that time. (Some say it's the most successful of all time!)

During the next two decades, Walt Disney Productions made wonderful movies that became classics. It expanded into television production. And it opened the world's first theme park. The name Disney became synonymous with creative family entertainment.

The Company That Whimpered

But after Walt died in 1966, the company started down a very bumpy road. Where Walt Disney Productions had once stood for innovation, it came to be marked by imitation—of its own past successes. Don Bluth, who left Disney in 1979, commented, "We felt like we were animating the same picture over and over again, with the faces changed a little."[1]

Instead of trying to look forward and break ground, Card Walker, who oversaw movie production, always asked himself, "What would Walt have done?" People at the studio began to joke morbidly, "We're working for a dead man."[2] The company cranked out more formula movies that didn't make a profit, and revenues continued to shrink. In 1981 the film division had an income of $34.6 million. In 1982 its income had fallen to $19.6 million. In 1983 it incurred a loss of $33.3 million. And the value of Disney stock was plummeting.

During that period, many American corporations were becoming victims of hostile takeovers, where Wall Street raiders would gain control of the company, cut it into pieces, and sell off its parts at a profit for themselves and their backers. Since Disney's stock value was down and it carried little debt, it became ripe for a hostile takeover.

In 1984, Disney narrowly avoided one takeover attempt and was facing the threat of yet another when its board of directors finally took a realistic look at where Disney stood. They decided that if the company was to survive, it would require radical changes, including something it had never done in its history—bringing in someone from outside Disney to run the company.

Getting Back into the Game

The people selected to turn around Disney were Michael Eisner as chairman and CEO and Frank Wells as president and COO. Concerning their challenging task, Eisner remarked,

> Our job wasn't to create something new, but to bring back the magic, to dress Disney up in more stylish clothes and expand its reach, to remind people why they loved the company in the first place . . . A brand is a living entity, and it is enriched or undermined cumulatively over time, the product of a thousand small gestures.[3]

Eisner was writing about his work on the Disney brand, but his remarks describe the approach he and Wells took to revitalizing the entire company. That involved a variety of strategies.

For one thing, they changed the name of the organization from Walt Disney Productions to the Walt Disney Company, reflecting the diversity of its interests. They brought together all of the organization's corporate executives and division heads for a weekly lunch to promote cohesiveness and to share ideas across divisions. They also hired key leaders, such as Jeffrey Katzenberg, to run their movie and television operations.

GOAL!

In a matter of a few years, Disney once again became a vital player in the entertainment industry. The almost-dead television division produced hits such as *The Golden Girls* and *Home Improvement.* The movie division, which had recently produced few movies and lost so much money, produced more movies in greater volume, with twenty-seven of its first thirty-three turning a profit. Before long, the company had four movie divisions: Disney, Touchstone, Hollywood Pictures, and Miramax. In late 1987, Disney became the number one studio at the box office for the first time in its history. And the animation division once again set the pace for the industry by creating films such as *The Little Mermaid, Beauty and the Beast, Aladdin,* and *The Lion King.*

Eisner and Wells expanded the company's efforts into new areas. They increased land development and built numerous new hotels at Walt Disney World. In 1987 they also opened retail stores in malls for the first time. Four years later, Disney owned 125 stores, which were generating $300 million in annual revenue. And of course, they improved the theme parks through expansion, innovation, and strategic partnerships with people such as George Lucas and Steven Spielberg. When they took over the company in 1984, the parks generated income of $250 million. By 1990, their income reached $800 million.

In 2000, the Walt Disney Company had revenues of $25.4 billion with $2.9 billion in net income (more than double the figures from 1984).[4] Disney has done more than just turn itself around. It has become an entertainment giant and one of the most powerful corporations in the world. For many of the years when the company was struggling, its team members looked at its history and the memory of its dead founder to gauge what to do. What they needed to do was to look at the scoreboard. *The team can make adjustments when it knows where it stands.* Eisner and Wells brought that ability to the company. They understood and implemented the Law of the Scoreboard.

Underscoring the Scoreboard

Every "game" has its own rules and its own definition of what it means to win. Some teams measure their success in points scored; others in profits. Still others may look at the number of people they serve. But no matter what the game is, there is always a scoreboard. And if a team is to accomplish its goals, it has to know where it stands. It has to look at itself in light of the scoreboard.

> *If a team is to accomplish its goals, it has to know where it stands.*

Why is that so important? Because teams that succeed make adjustments to continually improve themselves and their situations. For example, think about how a football team approaches a game. Before the competition starts, the team spends a tremendous amount of time planning. Players study hours of game film. They spend days figuring out what their opponent is likely to do, and they decide the best way to win. They come up with a detailed game plan.

As the game begins, the game plan is very important, and the scoreboard means nothing. But as the game goes on, the game plan means less and less, and the scoreboard becomes more and more significant. Why? Because the game is constantly changing. You see, the game plan tells what you *want* to happen. But the scoreboard tells what *is* happening.

Why the Scoreboard?

No team can ignore the reality of its situation and win. For years, Disney clung tenaciously to an out-of-date game plan while the world and the entertainment industry kept changing around it. The Disney team never really gave a hard look at the scoreboard. As a result they kept losing. That's what happens when you ignore the Law of the Scoreboard.

For any kind of team, the scoreboard is essential in the following ways:

1. The Scoreboard Is Essential to Understanding

In sports, players, coaches, and fans understand the importance of the scoreboard. That's why it is so visible at every stadium, arena, and ball field. The scoreboard provides a snapshot of the game at any given time. Even if you arrive at a game halfway into it, you can look at the scoreboard and assess the situation well.

> *The scoreboard provides a snapshot of the game at any given time.*

I'm often surprised by how many people outside sports try to succeed without a scoreboard. Some families operate their households without budgets, yet wonder why they are in debt. Some small-business owners go year after year without tracking sales or creating a balance sheet and wonder why they can't grow the business. Some pastors busy themselves with worthy activities, but never stop to measure whether they are reaching people or performing according to biblical standards.

2. The Scoreboard Is Essential to Evaluating

I believe that personal growth is a key to success. That's why I've taught lessons on growth at conferences and in books for more than twenty years. A key principle I teach is this:

Growth = Change

This sounds overly simple, doesn't it? But people sometimes lose sight of the fact that they cannot grow and remain the same at the same time. Most people are in a position that could be described by something Coach Lou Holtz once said: "We aren't where we want to be; we aren't where we ought to be; but thank goodness we aren't where we used to be."

But when it comes to growth, change alone is not enough. If you want to become better, you have to change in the right direction. You can do that only if you are able to evaluate yourself and your teammates. That is another reason for the scoreboard. It gives you continual feedback. Competing without a scoreboard is like bowling without pins. You may be working hard, but you don't really know how you're doing.

3. The Scoreboard Is Essential to Decision Making

Once you've evaluated your situation, you're ready to make decisions. In football, the quarterback uses information from the scoreboard to decide what play to call. In baseball, the scoreboard helps the manager know when to bring in a relief pitcher. In basketball, it can be used to determine whether to call a timeout.

That was the case at Disney. First Eisner looked at the company to understand its overall position. Then he evaluated individual areas for their effectiveness. Only then was he able to make sound decisions concerning how to get Disney back into the game.

4. The Scoreboard Is Essential to Adjusting

The higher the level on which you and your team are competing, the smaller the adjustments become to achieve your best. But making key adjustments is the secret to winning, and the scoreboard helps you to see where the adjustments need to be made.

One of the people on my staff is employing a unique scoreboard to help him make the adjustments required to go to the next level. That person is Kevin Small, the president of INJOY. Kevin is a real go-getter with high energy and enthusiasm. Being a young leader, he also has weak areas he needs to work on. To help him with that, he has engaged a personal coach to advise him, to help him read the scoreboard in his life, and to hold him accountable for growth. And it's really helping him. The small adjustments Kevin is making are taking him to another level and moving him closer to fulfilling his already tremendous potential.

5. The Scoreboard Is Essential to Winning

In the end, nobody can win without the scoreboard. How do you know when the game is on the line without the scoreboard? How do you know when time is running out unless you check the scoreboard? How will you know if it's cruise time or crunch time unless you have the scoreboard as a measuring device? If your desire is to take a leisurely drive with some friends, then you don't need to worry about a thing. But if you're trying to win the Indy 500, then you and your team *must* know how you're doing!

Some organizations view the scoreboard as a necessary evil. Others try to ignore it—something they cannot do for long and still do well in their profession. And some organizations make checking the scoreboard such an integral part of their culture that they are continually able to recognize and seize opportunities leading to huge success.

High Touch in a High-Tech World

That is certainly the case for eBay. I'm not a technical person. I don't have a computer—I don't even know how to use one—so I have not used eBay. I first heard about it from friends who are collectors. They talked about being able to find things they wanted through auctions held on the Internet. They seemed to be having fun with it, but to tell the truth I didn't pay much attention. Then I started seeing articles about eBay in the financial pages, and I read about the company's president and CEO, Meg Whitman.

Ebay is an e-commerce company that specializes in connecting buyers and sellers of goods on-line. It was founded by Pierre Omidyar in his San Jose, California, living room in September of 1995 with the idea of helping people find used, rare, or collectible items. The idea took off and became so successful that Omidyar soon recognized that he was in over his head. That's when he hired Meg Whitman, who had an MBA from Harvard and tremendous leadership experience as a general manager at Hasbro, president and CEO of FTD, and senior vice president of the Walt Disney Company.

An article in *Time* magazine explains eBay's success this way:

> As an online middleman between buyers and sellers, eBay is building an empire that bricks and mortar could not have touched. "If Buy.com goes down, you can still go to Circuit City," says Meg Whitman, . . . CEO of eBay. But if eBay crashes, there's nowhere else to go. And because eBay's job is connecting people—not selling them things—it isn't lumbered with a traditional retailing cost structure . . . "Ebay is the only e-tailer that really fulfills the promise of the Web," says Faye Landes, an e-commerce analyst at Sanford C. Bernstein & Co.[5]

The real genius of eBay is its mastery of the Law of the Scoreboard. It constantly makes adjustments because it knows where it stands, and that is what keeps it ahead. In the case of eBay, the scoreboard is the desires and interests of its customers—and potential customers. Sensing that many people are uneasy with conducting monetary transactions on the Internet, eBay made trust, safety, and privacy hallmarks of the company. Knowing that people wanted to get specific feedback on the individuals selling merchandise on the site, eBay created a unique rating system that allows subscribers to exchange information. The company even created a special Consumer Insights Group to track what people want.

Learning from the Customer

Over the last three years, eBay has learned everything it can about its users and what they want while keeping its finger on the pulse of larger consumer trends. The company has expanded from being a place to trade Beanie Babies to a multifaceted auction service that offers among other services:

- Special local trading for difficult-to-ship items
- Global auction service that covers 150 countries (including a strong presence in Europe)
- A business-to-business exchange for products and services
- An automobile auction site
- Real estate services

And in 2000, when eBay saw that a new start-up company called Half.com was thriving by selling used CDs, books, movies, and video games at set prices, eBay bought the company and added it to its holdings.[6]

The result is that eBay has received highly favorable recognition and hundreds of awards, including *Business Week* Entrepreneur of the Year, E-Retailer of the Year Award from *E-Retailer,* and a place on the list of *Forbes* magazine's one hundred most dynamic companies in America. In 2000, it had 22.5 million registered users, controlled 80 percent of the on-line auction market, and had revenues of $430 million (up 92 percent from 1999).

While other Internet-based companies are struggling to survive and searching for ways to finally make a profit, eBay seems poised to keep growing—and winning. Why? Because the eBay team always has an eye on the scoreboard. And *the team can make adjustments when it knows where it stands.* That's the Law of the Scoreboard.

Teamwork Thought

When you know what to do, then you can do what you know.

Becoming a Better Team Member

What is the scoreboard in your business or field? How do you measure your progress? Is it the bottom line? Is it the number of people you reach? Is it the level of excellence or innovation with which you do your work? How do you keep score?

> *When you know what to do, then you can do what you know.*

Take some time to identify how your team keeps score. Write the criteria here:

____

____

____

____

Now think about how you should be measuring yourself individually. What should you be keeping track of to make sure you are doing your best? Write the criteria here:

____

____

____

____

Becoming a Better Team Leader

If you lead the team, you have primary responsibility for checking the scoreboard and communicating the team's situation to its members. That doesn't necessarily mean you have to do it all by yourself. But you do need to make sure that team members continually evaluate, adjust, and make decisions as quickly as possible. That's the key to winning.

Do you have a system to make sure that happens? Or do you generally rely on your intuition? Using intuition is fine—as long as you have some fail-safe backups to make sure you don't let the team down.

Evaluate how consistently and effectively you consult your scoreboard. If you're not doing it as well as you should, then create a system that helps you to do it or empowers the leaders on your team to share the responsibility.

COMPANION ONLINE RESOURCE

Learn more about how the Law of the Scoreboard uniquely applies to you.

Take the FREE Law of the Scoreboard assessment at **LawsOfTeamwork.com**.

12

THE LAW OF THE BENCH

Great Teams Have Great Depth

Have you ever heard the expression "It's not over until the fat lady sings," or Yogi Berra's famous comment, "It ain't over till it's over"? Would you be surprised to know that sometimes it *is* over before it's over—and you can know when that is if you know the Law of the Bench?

Let me give you an example. One Saturday in September of 2000, I went to a football game with some friends: Kevin Small, the president of INJOY; Chris Goede, who used to play professional ball; and Steve Miller, my wonderful son-in-law. We were looking forward to an exciting game between the Georgia Tech Yellow Jackets and the Florida State Seminoles, even though FSU was a very strong favorite. There's an intense rivalry between all Georgia and Florida college teams, so the teams can get pretty pumped up.

And on that day, we weren't disappointed. The teams were battling, and the score was close. Tech was playing its heart out.

Only a Matter of Time

But as the third quarter came to a close, I said, "Come on, guys. This one is over." I sometimes leave games early because I hate to be stuck in traffic. Of course, if a game is really close or is likely to have some historic significance (such as a no-hitter in baseball), I stay to the end. On that day, the guys were surprised by my desire to leave, especially since the game was close and Tech had finally pulled ahead, 15 to 12.

"You don't want to see the end of the game?" asked Chris, a little curious.

"No, this game is over," I said. "Let's go to the car."

On our way back, we talked about it. It's true that Tech was hanging in there against FSU, especially when it came to the way the Yellow Jackets were playing defense. That was no easy task because the Seminoles had a powerful offense. But I had noticed throughout the course of the game that while Tech's starters were still in the game, FSU had been substituting many players from the bench—and the team's level of play had not been negatively affected. Because of that, I knew it was only a matter of time before Tech's players would be worn down by the powerful bench of FSU. And sure enough, the final score was 26 to 21 with FSU on top. That's the impact of the Law of the Bench. *Great teams have great depth.*

> *A great starter alone is simply not enough if a team wants to go to the highest level.*

The Role of the Bench

It's not difficult to see the importance of having well-trained, capable reserve players who sit on the bench in sports. In major-league baseball, the teams who win championships do so because they have more than just a good pitching rotation and solid fielding. They possess a bull pen with strong players who can substitute or pinch-hit off the bench. In the NBA, players and fans have long recognized the impact of the bench by talking about the all-important sixth man, the person who makes a significant contribution to the team's success yet isn't one of the five starters on the basketball court. And today's professional football coaches express the need to have two highly skilled quarterbacks capable of winning games on their teams. A great starter alone is simply not enough if a team wants to go to the highest level.

Any team that wants to excel must have good substitutes as well as starters. That's true in any field, not just sports. You may be able to do some wonderful things with a handful of top people, but if you want your team to do well over the long haul, you've got to build your bench. A great team with no bench eventually collapses.

Defining the Bench

In sports, it's easy to define which people are the starters and which make up the bench. But how do you define them in other fields? I want to suggest the following definitions:

> *Starters* are frontline people who directly add value to the organization or who directly influence its course.

The bench is made up of the people who indirectly add value to the organization or who support the starters.

A team's starters are the people most often in the spotlight, and as a result, they get most of the credit, and the people on the bench are liable to be neglected or overlooked. In fact, the people most likely to discount or discredit the contribution of the bench may be the starters. Some key players enjoy reminding the substitutes that they are "riding the pine." But any starter who minimizes the contribution of the bench is self-centered, underestimates what it takes for a team to be a success, and doesn't understand that *great teams have great depth.*

A leader who truly understood the Law of the Bench was UCLA's John Wooden, the "Wizard of Westwood," whose teams won ten college basketball national championships. Coach Wooden valued every person on his teams and the contribution that each person made. No coach did a better job of keeping his teams playing at the highest level over the long haul than Wooden. He observed, "Unselfishness is a trait I always insisted upon. I believed that every basketball team is a unit, and I didn't separate my players as to starters and subs. I tried to make it clear that every man plays a role, including the coach, the assistants, the trainer and the managers."[1]

The Bench Is Indispensable

Every human being has value, and every player on a team adds value to the team in some way. These truths alone should be enough to make team members care about the bench players. But there are also more specific reasons to honor and develop the players who may not be considered starters. Here are several:

1. Today's Bench Players May Be Tomorrow's Stars

Rare are the people who begin their careers as stars. And those who do sometimes find that their success is like that of some child actors. After a brief flash in the pan, they are never able to recapture the attention they got early on.

Most successful people go through an apprenticeship or period of seasoning. Look at someone like quarterback Joe Montana, who was inducted into the NFL Hall of Fame in 2000. He spent two years on the bench as a backup before being named the San Francisco 49ers starter. And as he was breaking records and leading his team to numerous Super Bowls, the person who sat on the bench as a backup to him was Steve Young, another top-notch quarterback.

> *Every human being has value, and every player on a team adds value to the team in some way.*

Some talented team members are recognized early for their positive potential and are groomed to succeed. Others labor in obscurity for years, learning, growing, and gaining experience. Then after a decade of hard work, they become "overnight successes." With the way people like to move from job to job today—and even from career to career—good leaders should always keep their eyes open for emerging talent. Never be in a hurry to pigeonhole anyone on your team as a nonstarter. Given the right encouragement, training, and opportunities, nearly anyone who has the desire has the potential to emerge someday as an effective player.

2. The Success of a Supporting Player Can Multiply the Success of a Starter

When every team member fulfills the role that best suits his talents, gifts, and experience and excels in that role, then the team really hums. The achievement of the whole team makes the starters flourish, and the achievement of the starters makes the team flourish. The whole team really is greater than the sum of its parts. Or to put it the way John Wooden did: "The main ingredient of stardom is the rest of the team."

> *"The main ingredient of stardom is the rest of the team."*
>
> —JOHN WOODEN

You have probably seen teams led by people who don't understand this truth. For example, they have million-dollar salespeople spending half of their time bogged down in paperwork rather than making calls on potential clients. If the organization would hire someone who enjoyed administrative tasks, not only would the salespeople be happier and more productive, but the gains in sales would more than make up for the cost of that support person.

We follow this rule at ISS, my company that provides consulting to churches for fund-raising. We employ consultants whose skills and backgrounds are truly one in a million. They work with hundreds of individual churches out in the field every year, and that is where they need to be to use their strengths. However, each consulting job requires numerous letters, instruction manuals, and other printed materials. And to accomplish that, ISS employs a team of talented support people who do a fabulous job with that work. When each person is allowed to work in an area of strength, the entire team wins.

3. There Are More Bench Players Than Starters

If you read through the roster of any successful team, you will see that the starters are always outnumbered by the other players on the team. In professional basketball, twelve people are on the team, but only five start. Major-league baseball teams start nine but carry forty players. In pro football, twenty-two people start on offense and defense, but each team is allowed to have fifty-three players in all. (College teams often have more than one hundred!)

You find similar situations in every field. In the entertainment industry, the actors are often known, but the hundreds of crew members necessary to make a movie aren't. In ministry, everyone recognizes the people up front during a worship service, but it takes scores of people working behind the scenes to bring that service together. For any politician or corporate executive or big-name fashion designer that you know about, there are hundreds of people toiling quietly in the background to make the person's work possible. Nobody can neglect the majority of the team and hope to be successful.

4. A Bench Player Placed Correctly Will at Times Be More Valuable Than a Starter

I think if you asked most people how they would classify administrative assistants as team members, they would tell you that they consider them to be bench players since their primary role is support. I would agree with that—although in some cases, administrative people have direct influence on an organization.

Take, for example, my assistant, Linda Eggers. Over the years, Linda has done just about everything at INJOY. She has been the company's bookkeeper. She used to run our conferences. She did marketing and product development. She is a very talented person. I think Linda is capable of doing just about anything. But she has chosen to take a supporting role as my assistant. And in that position, she makes a huge impact. Today my company has more than two hundred employees. I respect and value all of them. But if I lost everything tomorrow and I could keep only five or six people with whom to start over from scratch, Linda would be one of the people I would fight to keep. Her value as a support person makes her a starter.

5. A Strong Bench Gives the Leader More Options

When a team has no bench, the only option of its leader is moving the starters around to maximize their effectiveness. If a starter can't perform, the team is out of luck. When a team has a weak bench, the leader has a few options, but they are often not very good. But when a team has a great bench, the options are almost endless.

> *When a team has a great bench, the options are almost endless.*

That's why someone like Bobby Bowden, the coach at FSU, was able to wear down Georgia Tech. If one of his players got hurt, he had someone to replace him. If his opponent changed defenses, he had offensive players in reserve to overcome the challenge. No matter what kind of situation he faced, with a strong bench he had options that would give the team a chance to win.

6. The Bench Is Usually Called Upon at Critical Times for the Team

When an army is in trouble, what does it do? It calls up the reserves. That's the way it is in every area of life. You don't need the bench when things are going well; you need it when things aren't going well. When the starter gets hurt and the game is in jeopardy, a substitute steps in. That person's effectiveness often determines the team's success.

If your team is experiencing a tough time, then you know the importance of having a good bench. But if you are experiencing a smooth period, then now is the time to develop your backup players. Build the bench today for the crisis you will face tomorrow.

TODAY'S ACTIONS BUILD TOMORROW'S TEAM

As you think about the starters and the bench players on your team, recognize that the future of your team can be predicted by three things:

1. Recruitment: Who Is Joining the Team?

Adlai E. Stevenson offered this advice: "There are only three rules of sound administration: Pick good men, tell them not to cut corners, and back them to the limit; and picking good men is the most important." You cannot build a winning team without good players.

When it comes to recruiting, there are really only two kinds: You find the player for the position, or you find the position for the player. In the first situation, you have a position open, and you look for someone to fill that position. That is the typical way most recruiting works. But sometimes even when you don't have a position open, you find a potential player who is so good that you simply cannot pass up the opportunity to get him on the team.

I was in the second situation last year. When I discovered that John Hull might be interested in coming to work for The INJOY Group, I didn't have a specific position for him. But he is such a high-impact player that I brought him aboard. And in a matter of a few months, he became the president of EQUIP, the nonprofit organization I founded, when its original president, Ron McManus, desired to lead another department for me. If I hadn't asked John to come aboard when I did, the team might have missed out on a wonderful leader.

2. Training: Are You Developing the Team?

You cannot solve tomorrow's problems with today's solutions. If you want the team to succeed as it meets new challenges, you have to prepare it. That means helping starters to maximize their potential and training the people on the bench to become starters when their time comes.

> *You cannot solve tomorrow's problems with today's solutions.*

If you have leadership responsibility for your team, then take the initiative to make sure everyone on the team is growing and improving.

3. Losses: Who Is Leaving the Team?

The only place that never loses people is the cemetery. Losing team members is inevitable. But the good news is that you can choose the members you lose. If you keep nonproductive people, the productive ones become frustrated and leave. If you remove the people who don't add value, then the whole team gets better. It's just like trimming trees: If you don't cut the deadwood, eventually the whole tree falls. But if you remove the deadwood, the tree becomes healthier, the healthy branches produce more, and there's room for productive new branches on the tree.

The best way to describe how to grow and improve the team

and its bench is what I call the revolving door principle. Here's the way it works: A team will always have gains and losses. People are constantly coming into an organization while others leave it. The key to its future success is gaining a more effective person with each loss.

Let's say, for example, that you can rate every person's effectiveness on a scale of 1 to 10, with 10 as the highest. As the revolving door turns, if your team is losing 4s but gaining 8s, then your future looks bright. If you're losing 8s and gaining 4s, then the future looks bleak. And if you're losing 4s and gaining other 4s, then you're wearing your team out with activity but making no progress.

Phases of an Organization and Its Revolving Door

Any team that is avoiding stagnation by trying to improve will go through changes, and as the revolving door moves, different kinds of people will come and go during various phases. For example, when an organization is new and just getting started, it recruits strongly. It has no one to lose and is glad to gain anyone. The good news is that as people come on board, a team is being formed. The bad news is that the people the team is gaining are not always good.

When a team asks for commitment, some team members leave the team. But that's good. Commitment drives away the uncommitted, while it makes those who stay even stronger in the commitment they already possess.

Once the team has a committed core and begins to grow, it again gains people. The people who join the team are often attracted to it because of the level of commitment they see in existing players. That

Type of Team	Gain or Loss	Nature of Loss or Gain
New Team	More Gains Than Losses	Gains Are Not Always Positive
Committed Team	More Losses Than Gains	Losses Are Positive
Growing Team	More Gains Than Losses	Gains Are Positive
Successful Team	More Losses Than Gains	Losses Are Not Positive
Legacy Team	More Gains Than Losses	Gains Are Positive

builds the team's ability and drives it to achieve—and leads to its success.

However, once a team becomes successful, some members will want to leave to try to find greater success on their own. That's a critical time for a team. If you can give people intriguing challenges and share both responsibilities and rewards with them, you may be able to persuade them to stay. (If you can't, you'll probably have to rely on your backup players, and then you'll find out what kind of bench you've built!)

If you can sustain growth in the midst of success and repeat the process while continually building your bench, then you can create a legacy team. That's what organizations such as General Electric, Disney, and Home Depot have done. Their sustained growth and reputations for success continue to draw good people to them.

Who Is Your MVP?

The key to making the most of the Law of the Bench is to continually improve the team. As you bring on better players, first improve your starters. Then build your bench. Do that long enough and you will build a great team because *great teams have great depth.* That's the Law of the Bench.

Building a great team is a process that takes a tremendous amount of work, and the bigger the organization gets, the harder the task becomes. I'm acutely aware of that because in the last three and a half years, The INJOY Group has grown from less than fifty people to more than two hundred! When you're experiencing that kind of explosive growth, your HR person may be your MVP.

> *The key to making the most of the Law of the Bench is to continually improve the team.*

Let me tell you about the person most responsible for keeping the revolving door moving in the right direction in my company. Her name is Stacy Buchanan. Two and a half years ago, an acquaintance of hers who was a headhunter directed her to The INJOY Group. At the time, we were looking for a senior accountant, and Stacy had an extensive background in accounting, having done much of the groundwork to become a CPA. She had also worked for six years at an internationally known nonprofit organization and spent several years teaching.

Bold Move

Stacy believed with all her heart that she belonged at The INJOY Group, and she really wanted to work with us. So she came in and interviewed with us. But the last thing in the world she wanted to do was go back into accounting. Christine Johnson, a longtime INJOY employee who was functioning as our HR manager at the time, was interviewing Stacy. Christine could tell that she was an "eagle" and didn't want her to get away. So she introduced Stacy to the COO, Dick Peterson. As they talked, he, too, could tell she was a tremendous catch. Finally he asked her, "What do you want to do?"

Stacy gathered her courage and replied, "To tell you the truth, Dick, I want Christine's job: recruiting."

That was music to Christine's ears. She was dutifully recruiting new employees, but she didn't really enjoy it—nor did it utilize her greatest strengths. She and Dick were happy to create a position for Stacy as a recruiter, thus freeing Christine to focus on administration and management. In the thirty months since then, Stacy has hired nearly two hundred people for the company—both starters and bench players. And she does a fantastic job.

"I know I am going to sound like a preacher with my six Ps," says Stacy, "but this will give you an idea of how I place people. I analyze the following areas:

1. *Personality:* I use the DISC test, a diagnostic tool that indicates whether someone's personality is driving, influencing, supporting, or calculating.
2. *Passion:* I find out what motivates them—results, relationships, money, recognition, affirmation, impact, or security.
3. *Pattern:* I look for patterns in their successes and their failures. I figure out whether they work best alone or on a team.
4. *Potential:* I try to see what they might accomplish given the

right direction, motivation, coaching, and leadership. I particularly gauge whether they are maintainers or builders.

5. *Profile:* I gauge whether they will fit our culture and whether they are really INJOY material.
6. *Placement:* Finally I try to measure where they fit—which team will both benefit from them and add value to them.

Stacy has done a wonderful job of building our team through recruiting. And now she has expanded her role into the area of training. She has played an instrumental role in starting the nine mentoring groups that are currently in place at The INJOY Group. Stacy summarizes her work by saying, "My desire is to see people play the music that is contained in their souls."

If you want your team to become the very best it can be, then you need to concentrate on the people you're gaining, the ones you're losing, and the ones you're developing. That's the only way to build a great team. It has to be solid at every level. And never lose sight of the Law of the Bench. Remember, *great teams have great depth.*

Teamwork Thought

Better players make you a better player.

Becoming a Better Team Member

How would you define yourself: a bench player or a starter? If you are on the bench, then your job is to do two things: Help the starters to shine, and prepare yourself to be a starter in the future. You can do that by cultivating an attitude of service and teachability, and by doing whatever you can to learn and grow.

If you are a starter, then you should perform at your best for the sake of the team, and you should honor the people on the bench. You do that by acknowledging the value of their contribution and by helping prepare them to start someday. If you are not already mentoring a teammate on the bench, start doing so right away.

Becoming a Better Team Leader

If you lead your team, you are responsible for making sure the revolving door moves in such a way that the players who are joining the team are better than those who are leaving. One way you can facilitate that is to place high value on the good people already on the team.

Every team has three groups of players. In this chapter I described the *starters,* who directly add value to the organization or who directly influence its course, and the *bench players,* who indirectly add value to the organization or who support the starters. The third group is a core group within the starters that I call the *inner-circle members.* Without these people the team would fall apart. Your job is to make sure each group is continually developed so that bench players are able to step up to become starters, and starters are able to step up to become inner-circle members.

If you're not sure who the inner-circle members are on your team, then try this exercise: Write the names of the people on your team who are starters. Now determine the people you could most easily do without. One by one, check off the names of the people whose loss would hurt the team least if they left. At some point you will end up with a smaller group of people without whom the team would be dead. That's your inner circle. (You can even rank the remaining people in order of importance.)

It's a good exercise to remind you of the value of people on the team. And by the way, if your treatment of those people doesn't match their value, you run the risk of losing them and having your revolving door work against you.

COMPANION ONLINE RESOURCE

Learn more about how the Law of the Bench uniquely applies to you.

Take the FREE Law of the Bench assessment at **LawsOfTeamwork.com**.

13

THE LAW OF IDENTITY

Shared Values Define the Team

At least one day a year, I try to bring together everyone in my organization. Early in INJOY's history, that was easy. Back in 1985 when we founded the company, Dick Peterson, who is now the company's COO, and I could get together on a moment's notice with his mother-in-law, Erma (our only employee), and the four or five volunteers who helped us (two of whom were our wives). Even ten years later we were still a fairly small outfit. The entire company could meet around one large conference table.

Today things are different. Now we have to rent a hall to accommodate all of our employees, but we still make the effort to get together. In fact, it's more important for us to do that now than it ever was before. Because of our size and the diversity of operations, the people on our team have a tendency to get disconnected from one another. And it becomes increasingly difficult for the leaders in the organization to maintain a personal connection with everyone.

Defining the Team

Maybe you've experienced the disconnectedness that often accompanies rapid growth in an organization. Granted, with slightly more than two hundred employees, ours is not a large company, but it is big enough to experience growing pains. Where the team was once defined almost entirely through relationships, it now needs something more to keep it together. That's where the Law of Identity comes into play: *Shared values define the team.* Even if some members of a team don't share common experiences or have a personal relationship with one another, they can possess a cohesiveness that defies the size of the team. What it takes is a common vision (the Law of the Compass) and shared values. If everyone embraces the same values, team members can still have a connection to one another and to the larger team.

> *Just as personal values influence and guide an individual's behavior, organizational values influence and guide the team's behavior.*

We've all seen teams that have a common goal yet lack common values. Everyone on the team has different ideas about what's important. The result is chaos. Eventually the team breaks down if everyone tries to do things his own way. That's why team members need to be on the same page. Just as personal values influence and guide an individual's behavior, organizational values influence and guide the team's behavior.

THE VALUE OF VALUES

Values can help a team to become more connected and more effective. Shared values are like . . .

Glue

When difficult times come—and they do for every team—values hold people together. Look at a marriage, for example. It's easy for a couple to stay together when they are feeling the flush of love and everything is going smoothly. But eventually the passion that drew them together fades. And adversity comes. What keeps the people who stay married together? It's their values. Their values are more important than their feelings. They value their marriage so highly that they are willing to fight *for* the relationship. If two people don't have that mind-set going into the wedding, then their chances of staying together are pretty slim.

The same is true for any other team. If the players don't know what their values are—and live them out—their chances of working as a unit and reaching their potential are very small.

A Foundation

All teams need stability to perform well and to grow. Values provide a stable foundation that makes those things possible. This is true for just about any kind of relationship to grow. For example, if you are trying to build a relationship with someone from another culture, you begin by looking for the things you have in common. If you are trying to make a sale with a new customer, you look for common ground. The same is true when it comes to team building. You need something to build on, and values make the strongest foundation.

A Ruler

Values also help set the standard for a team's performance. In the corporate world, the values are often expressed in a mission statement or set of guidelines for doing business. But sometimes a company's stated values and its real values don't match up.

> *Values help set the standard for a team's performance.*

Author and management expert Ken Blanchard emphasizes, "Lots of companies claim they have a set of core values, but what they mean is a list of generic business beliefs that everyone would agree with, such as having integrity, making a profit, and responding to customers. Such values have meaning only when they are further defined in terms of how people actually behave and are rank-ordered to reveal priority." And they function as a measure of expectations and performance when they are genuinely embraced.

A Compass

Do you remember the television show *Dallas* from the 1980s? The main character was J. R. Ewing, a notoriously dishonest businessman. His character code for living can be summarized by something he said in an episode of the show: "Once you give up your ethics, the rest is a piece of cake." To a person with no values, anything goes.

I think we live in a time when people are searching for standards to live by. When individuals embrace strong values, they possess a moral compass that helps them make decisions. The same is true for people in an organization. When the team identifies and embraces a set of values, then in a month, a year, or a decade, no matter how much circumstances change or what challenges present themselves, people on the team still know it's moving in the right direction and make good decisions.

A Magnet

A team's values attract people with like values to the team. Think about some of the teams we've examined in previous chapters. What kinds of people are drawn to Habitat for Humanity? People who want to see substandard housing eliminated. What kinds of people are attracted to Enron? People who value innovation and organizational flexibility.

In *The 21 Irrefutable Laws of Leadership,* the Law of Magnetism states, "Who you are is who you attract." That law is as true for teams as it is for leaders. People attract other like-minded people.

An Identity

Values define the team and give it a unique identity—to team members, potential recruits, clients, and the public. What you believe identifies who you are.

THE VALUES OF THE INJOY GROUP

When I brought together all of the employees of The INJOY Group for our annual meeting this year, I wanted to emphasize our values. I think our team members see them acted out every day, but I wanted to give everyone a common language for the values to help ensure our alignment with them. To do that, I taught a lesson on those values.

Communication of the team's values is the place to start with the Law of Identity. A team cannot share values if the values have not been shared with the team. Allow me to acquaint you with the six core values that I shared with The INJOY Group so that you have a sense of what I mean.

1. The Personal Growth of Each Team Member

I am a strong believer in potential. Every day I work to develop my own, and I encourage everyone in my sphere of influence to do the same. How do people work to develop their potential? They start by making personal growth a priority.

Personal growth has been a major theme of my life. When I was a kid, my father used to pay me and my siblings to read books that would improve us. He also sent us to conferences. As I got older, reading books, listening to instructional tapes, and attending conferences became regular practices for me. Later, as I sought the key to organizational growth, I discovered another reason to promote personal growth because I found that the way to grow any organization is to grow the people in that organization.

> *A team cannot share values if the values have not been shared with the team.*

To promote personal growth in my organization, we encourage people to become members of a mentoring group. We also send people to our own conferences and to other types of training. We provide books, tapes, and other personal-growth tools. And I personally spend time every month mentoring and developing the top leaders of the organization. When we or an employee discovers that the person would flourish in a different position or division of the company, we encourage him to explore new possibilities and make a change. You can't stand in the way of your employees' growth and still hope to grow your organization.

2. The Priority of Adding Value to Others

The INJOY Group exists to add value to people. That is our primary mission. First, we do that with the people in our own organization. But we also do it for our customers and clients. It's the reason we develop and provide consulting, training, and resources to organizations and individuals across the country and around the world. The day we can't add value to people is the day we close our doors.

3. The Power of Partnership

One of my favorite quotes comes from Mother Teresa, who observed, "You can do what I cannot do. I can do what you cannot do. Together we can do great things." That's a succinct way to describe partnership.

> *"You can do what I cannot do. I can do what you cannot do. Together we can do great things."*
>
> —MOTHER TERESA

It took me almost forty years to discover that I can't do everything. (You probably learned that sooner than I did; my high energy, low IQ, and endless optimism got the better of me for years!) That's when I realized the power of partnership. Over the years, our organization has learned more and more about working with others. Now partnership is the way we choose to accomplish our mission. Dave Sutherland, the CEO of The INJOY Group, likes to remind everyone, "Partnership begins the moment that a leader realizes we add value to him, and it ends when his vision is accomplished."

In recent years, we have expanded our partnership to include strategic alliances with other organizations. These partnerships have enabled The INJOY Group to train thousands of leaders in nearly a dozen countries overseas and to give away tens of thousands of books every year to people in developing countries.

I've come up with an acronym that describes what partnership means to me. As your partner, we promise to . . .

Put your needs first in every situation.

Add value to your personal leadership.

Recognize we serve a common goal.

Tailor our services to meet your need.

Never take for granted the trust placed in us.

Embody excellence in everything we do.

Respect everyone's uniqueness.

As individuals and as an organization, we can be good partners if we can remember each element.

4. The Practice of Raising Up and Developing Leaders

Everything rises and falls on leadership. That's why I have dedicated the past twenty years of my life to teaching leadership. That's also why I spend so much time finding and developing leaders. The single greatest way to impact an organization is to focus on leadership development. There is almost no limit to the potential of an organization that recruits good people, raises them up as leaders, and continually develops them.

> *The single greatest way to impact an organization is to focus on leadership development.*

5. The Proper Stewardship of the Organization

Any organization that wants to continue fulfilling its mission must learn to be a good steward of its resources. There are three primary ways we do that in our company: managing our assets to get the most out of them, placing our people strategically so they can give and receive as much as possible, and giving of ourselves to worthy causes. If we can do all three of these things, then we are maximizing the use of all the resources we have.

6. The Purpose of Glorifying God

The INJOY Group is an organization made up primarily of Christians, and our roots are in helping churches and pastors to reach their potential. Because of our heritage and our strong convictions, we believe that everything we do should honor God.

Undoubtedly the values of your organization will be different from ours. And that's as it should be. Your values should reflect the people on the team and their leader. What's important is that you go through the discovery process and embrace the team's values. Once you do, you will better understand your team, its mission, and its potential. Never forget that *shared values define the team.* That's the Law of Identity.

Values Add Value to Your Team

If you've never really thought about how your team's values can reveal its identity and increase its potential, go through the following process with your team:

- *Articulate the values.* Spend some think time or bring together a group of key team members to articulate the team's values. Then put them on paper.

- *Compare values with practices.* Then watch the team in action. You want to make sure the values you identify match the ones you're living. The alignment of the stated values and the behavior of team members boosts the team's energy and effectiveness. But if they are out of alignment, then the team will suffer.

- *Teach the values.* Once you settle what the right values are, you need to teach them to everyone on the team. Do it clearly, creatively, and continually.

- *Practice the values.* Values have no value if you don't put them into practice. If you discover teammates whose actions don't match the team's values, help them to make the changes necessary to align themselves with the rest of the team.

- *Institutionalize the values.* Weave the team's values into the fabric of the team. For example, my friend Bill Hybels, senior pastor of Willow Creek Community Church, identifies "community" as one of the core values of his church. To reinforce that value, the first third of every leadership meeting—whether it is staff, elders, or the board—is dedicated to building and maintaining the personal relationships among the members of that group.

- *Publicly praise the values.* The most fundamental management truth I've ever learned is that what gets rewarded gets done. If you praise and honor the people who epitomize the values of the team, those values get embraced and upheld by other members of the team. There is no better reinforcement.

If you are the leader of your team, it is especially important that you take your team through this process. Left to themselves, with no help to embrace the values you know to be fundamental, team members will create an identity of their choosing. For better or worse, the values of the most influential people on the team will become the team's values. However, by implementing each of the steps I outlined and continuing to repeat them over time, you will find that the culture of your organization will begin to change, and your people will embrace a new identity that you help them find. And once they develop a common team identity, they will work together better, even as the organization grows and changes.

> *The most fundamental management truth I've ever learned is that what gets rewarded gets done.*

No Place Like Home

When I moved to Atlanta, I became acquainted with an organization that has developed its unique identity and fosters a strong sense of teamwork despite being a huge company. That organization is Home Depot.

Now, I am not a do-it-yourselfer. What's the opposite of handy? Handless? Manually challenged? Whatever it is, that describes me. Then there's my son, Joel Porter. He never met a tool he didn't like, and if a thing can be fixed, he will find a way to do it. When he was thirteen years old, we let him create a workshop in a room adjacent to our garage. He put in a workbench, installed fixtures, and wired the room. A friend of ours who used to be a contractor said Joel had put enough power in that small room to light up an entire house!

After our arrival in Atlanta, Joel found himself a job at Home Depot, and he couldn't have been happier. Every day he would come home and tell us about the company, what he did that day, and the values the company held dear.

Intrigued, I did some research of my own. I discovered that the company was founded by Bernie Marcus and Arthur Blank. They opened their first store in Atlanta in June of 1979 after both men had been fired fourteen months earlier from Handy Dan, a home improvement chain located in the western part of the United States. For years, Marcus, a man with considerable retail experience and leadership talent, had possessed a vision for a national chain of huge one-stop home improvement stores. His idea was to offer the widest selection of products at the lowest prices with the best customer service possible.

Building Home Depot

Getting the company off the ground required the two men to keep plugging away, slowly expanding the business, opening more stores, and attracting first-rate people. Marcus said, "We are only as good as our people—especially the men and women working in our stores every day . . . That's why we believe a sure way of growing this company is to clearly state our values and instill them in our associates."[1]

The right leaders with the right values have attracted the right people to make the company a blockbuster. In 1979, they started with four stores. In 1999, Home Depot had 775 stores, 160,000 employees, and $38.4 billion in annual sales.[2]

Values truly are at the heart of Home Depot's success. Marcus explained,

> A set of eight values has been our bedrock for the past twenty years. Although they were not put in writing until 1995, these values—the basis for the way we run the company—enabled us to explode across the North American landscape and will be the vehicle for reaching our ambitious goals in the international marketplace . . .
>
> - *Excellent customer service.* Doing whatever it takes to build customer loyalty.
> - *Taking care of our people.* The most important reason for The Home Depot's success.
> - *Developing entrepreneurial spirit.* We think of our organizational structure as an inverted pyramid: Stores and customers are at the top and senior management is on the bottom.
> - *Respect for all people.* Talent and good people are everywhere, and we can't afford to overlook any source of good people.
> - *Building strong relationships with associates, customers, vendors and communities.*
> - *Doing the right thing, not just doing things right.*
> - *Giving back to our communities as an integral part of doing business.*
> - *Shareholder return.* Investors in The Home Depot will benefit from the money they've given us to grow our business.[3]

These values have made the company a great place for people to work. For example, from the day Home Depot opened, the company has offered employees stock options rather than bonuses. That kind of treatment has made more than one thousand of its employees millionaires!

Joel Porter has since left his job at Home Depot. He now works for The INJOY Group in a technical capacity as our studio production manager. But he will always have a heart for Home Depot. Why? Because the company has an identity he respects. It has *shared values, and the values define the team.* That's the impact their organization had on him, and that's the impact the Law of Identity can have on you and your team.

Teamwork Thought

If your values are the same as the team's, you become more valuable to the team.

Becoming a Better Team Member

If you want to add value to your team and help it reach its potential, then you need to share in its values. First, make sure that you know what they are. Then, examine your values and goals in comparison to them. If you can wholeheartedly buy into the team's values, commit yourself to aligning yourself with them. If you can't, then your misalignment will be a constant source of frustration to you and your teammates. And you might want to think about finding a different team.

BECOMING A BETTER TEAM LEADER

As the leader of an organization, you have responsibilities when it comes to the team's values. I recommend that you proceed by following these steps:

- Know the values that the team should embrace.
- Live the values.
- Communicate the values to the team.
- Obtain buy-in of the values through aligned behavior among teammates.

Remember, the process takes time. Getting your people to buy in can be especially difficult. But the better leader you are, the more quickly they will buy into you. And the more quickly they buy into you, the more rapidly they will buy into the values you communicate. (To explore this leadership concept in more depth, read the Law of Buy-In in *The 21 Irrefutable Laws of Leadership.*)

COMPANION
ONLINE
RESOURCE

Learn more about how the Law of Identity uniquely applies to you.

Take the FREE Law of Identity assessment at **LawsOfTeamwork.com**.

14

THE LAW OF COMMUNICATION

Interaction Fuels Action

When Gordon Bethune took over Continental Airlines in 1994, the company was a mess. It had suffered through ten changes in leadership in ten years. It had gone through bankruptcy proceedings twice. Its stock value was at a pitiful $3.25 a share. It had not made a profit in a decade. Customers were flocking away from the airline, and those who did use Continental were rarely happy because in the words of Bethune, their planes "came and went as they happened to" with no predictability. That's not what business travelers and vacationers are looking for in an airline!

TRYING TIMES FOR THE TEAM

In his book, *From Worst to First,* Bethune described the state of Continental when he arrived:

> In the years leading up to 1994, Continental was simply the worst among the nation's 10 biggest airlines . . . For example, DOT [the Department of Transportation] measures those 10 largest airlines in on-time percentage . . . *Continental was dead last.* It measures the number of mishandled-baggage reports filed per 1,000 passengers. *Continental was worst.* It measures the number of complaints it receives per 100,000 passengers on each airline. Continental was last. And not just last—in 1994, *Continental got almost three times as many complaints as the industry average* and more than 30 percent more complaints than the ninth-best airline, the runner-up in lousy service. We had a real lock on last place in that category . . . We weren't just the worst big airline. *We lapped the field.*[1]

When a company is that bad, the employees can't help being affected. Morale at Continental was abysmal. Cooperation was nonexistent. Communication was at an all-time low. Employees had been lied to so often and so thoroughly that they didn't believe anything they were told. According to Bethune, they had learned one survival strategy: Duck. "That's what I joined in 1994," commented Bethune, "a company with a lousy product, angry employees, low wages, a history of ineffective management, and, I soon learned, an incipient bankruptcy, our third, which would probably kill us."[2]

Trying to Turn Around the Team

Bethune's goal was to save Continental, but he knew that to do it, he would have to change the culture of the company. The key would be communication. He knew that positive interaction could turn the company around. If he could win the communication battle, he believed he could get the employees to work together again for the good of the team, the customers, and the stockholders.

His first step was to open up the executive offices to the rest of the team. When he began working for Continental, the twentieth-floor suite occupied by top management in Houston was like a fortress. Its doors were locked, the area was surveyed by lots of security cameras, and nobody could enter the area without a proper ID. It wasn't exactly inviting. Bethune literally propped open the doors and hosted open houses for employees to break down the intimidation factor between leaders and the rest of the team.

The next thing he did was to work to break the old bureaucracy that had developed over the years. At Continental, rules and manuals had taken the place of communication and the use of judgment. The chief symptom of that mind-set was the nine-inch-thick book of rules for employees that had come to be known as the "Thou Shalt Not" book. It was so detailed that it dictated what color pencil an agent was supposed to use on a boarding pass. In a significant gesture, CEO Bethune, along with Continental President Greg Brenneman, gathered employees in the parking lot, dropped the manual in a trash can, doused it with gasoline, and burned it![3] The message was clear. Everything at Continental was going to change.

Communication Culture

Continental didn't change overnight. In fact, as Bethune and Brenneman laid out their "Go Forward Plan," employees were skeptical. But the leaders kept meeting with the people, committed themselves to being honest with them, and maintained their patience. If the news was good, they told the people. If the news was bad, they still told them. They put up bulletin boards in every employee area that showed two things: (1) their ratings for the last year according to the Department of Transportation rating guidelines; and (2) daily news updates from the company. They created a weekly voice mail message to everyone on the team. They also put lots of communication in writing, using a monthly employee newsletter called *Continental Times and Continental Quarterly*, which they mailed to every employee's home. They put news wire–style LED displays by every coffee and soda machine. They even created 800-number hot lines for questions and information that could be accessed by any employee from anywhere in the world.

Bethune's communication policy was—and is—simple: "Unless it's dangerous or illegal for us to share it, we share it."

A company that had been characterized by distrust and lack of cooperation became a place where communication was pervasive. Bethune's communication policy was—and is—simple: "Unless it's dangerous or illegal for us to share it, we share it."[4] It took time, but eventually the company began to turn. Employees started to trust their leaders. They began to work with and trust one another. And for the first time in more than a decade, the employees of Continental functioned as a team.

Today, Continental's service is among the best in its industry. Employee morale is high. And the company is profitable. In 1994, the year Bethune took over, the company *lost* $204 million. In 1995, it made a *profit* of $202 million. The next year it doubled. As of April 2001, Continental had posted twenty-four consecutive profitable quarters in an industry where many of its competitors are struggling to stay in the black. The company's stock has split twice, and each share is worth more than ten times the value it had in 1994.

What's in a Word?

Communication wasn't the entire reason for Continental's success. But without good communication, the company most likely would have continued on autopilot right into its third (and final) bankruptcy. Creating positive change in an organization requires communication. *Interaction fuels action.* That is the power of the Law of Communication.

> *Effective teams have teammates who are constantly talking to one another.*

Only with good communication can a team succeed—it doesn't matter whether that team is a family, a company, a ministry, or a ball club. Effective teams have teammates who are constantly talking to one another. Communication increases commitment and connection; they in turn fuel action. If you want your team to *perform* at the highest level, the people on it need to be able to talk to and listen to one another.

Communication Matters

When people don't communicate effectively, the result can often be comical. Years ago, I came across the following illustration that conveys what I mean. It is made up of a series of memos on a college campus:

> **President to Academic V.P.:** Next Thursday Halley's Comet will appear over this area. This is an event which occurs only once every 75 years. Call the Division Heads and have them assemble their professors and students on the athletic field and explain this

phenomenon to them. If it rains, then cancel the observation and have the classes meet in the gym to see a film about the comet.

Academic V.P. to Division Chairmen: By order of the President, next Thursday Halley's Comet will appear over the athletic field. If it rains, then cancel classes and report to the gym with your professors and students where you will be shown films, a phenomenal event which occurs only once every 75 years.

Division Chairman to Professors: By order of the Phenomenal President, next Thursday Halley's Comet will appear in the gym. In case of rain over the athletic field the President will give another order, something which occurs every 75 years.

Professor to Students: Next Thursday the President will appear in our gym with Halley's Comet, something which occurs every 75 years. If it rains the President will cancel the comet and order us all out to our phenomenal athletic field.

Student Writing Home to Parents: When it rains next Thursday over the school athletic field, the phenomenal 75-year-old President will cancel all classes and appear before the whole school in the gym accompanied by Bill Halley and the Comets.

Scott Adams, the creator of the Dilbert comic strip, has masterfully described an organization where everyone does his best to undermine communication. The boss sends an employee to work for a year on a project that has been canceled, then later demotes the person for wasting so much time. Members of the marketing department continually think up harebrained products and promote them to the public; then they ask the engineers to produce them on an impossible timetable. The higher up in the organization people are, the more clueless they are. Thinkers are punished, the lazy are rewarded, and every decision is arbitrary. The comic strip is hilarious. What's sad is that too many American workers identify with it.

If you've ever been on a team where teammates never let one another know what's going on, then you know how frustrating poor communication can be. The team gets stuck because nobody knows what the real agenda is. Important tasks remain uncompleted because each of two team members believes the other one is taking care of it—or people duplicate others' work. Departments within the organization fight because each believes it is being sabotaged by the other.

In the book *Empowered Teams,* authors Richard Wellins, William Byham, and Jeanne Wilson state, "Communication refers to the style and extent of interactions both among members and between members and those outside the team. It also refers to the way that members handle conflict, decision making, and day-to-day interactions."

A Different Picture of Communication

An excellent example of the complexity—and importance—of good communication can be seen by watching a professional football team in the half minute prior to a play. When one play ends, the offensive team has only forty seconds to get itself ready for the next play. In that time, the quarterback first decides if there is enough time for the team to huddle. If there is, he calls the team members together and gives them the play. If there isn't, he communicates that he will call the play using a code at the line of scrimmage.

For many plays at the professional level, the team will line up with players in one formation and then move them around before the play to try to confuse the defense. If time is short, the quarterback will communicate to the players that they should skip the extra steps and just line up in the formation that will be used to run the play.

As the eleven offensive players approach the line, each is doing two things: assessing what the defense is doing, and paying attention to teammates for communication cues. The linemen who will be blocking pay attention to what kinds of players the other team has in the game and where they are positioned. The center, who hikes the ball to the quarterback, is usually responsible for calling out the blocking scheme to his teammates based on the defense.

Meanwhile, the quarterback is assessing the defense. If he thinks the play he has called in the huddle will fail against the defense, he is likely to use a few words to call an alternate play at the line of scrimmage. If the defense is lined up in such a way that the original play will work, but the blocking scheme of the running backs behind him is likely to fail, then he can change their blocking assignments.

At the same time, the quarterback, the running backs, and the receivers are watching the defense to see if they are about to do anything unusual, such as sending extra players after the quarterback to tackle him in a blitz. If the offensive players do see a blitz coming, then, without a word, the receivers and running backs change their assignments to a predetermined Plan B for that play, and they hope that everyone on the team made the same assessment.

Football is an extremely complex sport. The casual observer has no idea so much communication is going on before every play.

Sometimes it's subtle. Players call out things in code. They use hand signals. One player may simply point and communicate a lot of information to another teammate. And sometimes a quarterback and a receiver will just give each other a look and communicate enough information to make it possible for them to score on the play.

Communication on Your Team

Communication on your team may not look anything like what happens on a football field. But the success of your team and the ability of your team members to work together are just as dependent on good communication. Allow me to give you some guidelines that will help your team to improve in this area. Every team has to learn how to develop good communication in four areas.

> *"If I had to name a single all-purpose instrument of leadership, it would be communication."*
>
> —JOHN W. GARDNER

1. From Leader to Teammates

John W. Gardner observed, "If I had to name a single all-purpose instrument of leadership, it would be communication." Perhaps you are familiar with my books on leadership; then you know that I believe everything rises and falls on leadership. What I haven't mentioned before is that leadership rises and falls on communication. You must be able to communicate to lead others effectively.

If you lead your team, give yourself these standards to live by as you communicate to your people:

- *Be consistent.* Nothing frustrates team members more than leaders who can't make up their minds. One of the things that won the team over to Gordon Bethune was the consistency of his communication. His employees always knew they could depend on him and what he said.

- *Be clear.* Your team cannot execute if the members don't know what you want. Don't try to dazzle anyone with your intelligence; impress people with your straightforwardness.

- *Be courteous.* Everyone deserves to be shown respect, no matter what the position or what kind of history you might have with him. By being courteous to your people, you set the tone for the entire organization.

Never forget that because you are the leader, your communication sets the tone for the interaction among your people. Teams always reflect their leaders. And never forget that good communication is never one-way. It should not be top-down or dictatorial. The best leaders listen, invite, and then encourage participation.

2. From Teammates to Leader

Good team leaders never want yes-men. They want direct and honest communication from their people. Even autocratic movie mogul Sam Goldwyn quipped, "I want my people to speak up and be honest, even if it costs them their jobs."

I have always encouraged people on my team to speak openly and directly with me. When we hold meetings, they are often brainstorming sessions where the best idea wins. Often, a team member's remarks or observations really help the team. Sometimes we disagree. That's okay because we've developed strong enough relationships that we can survive conflict. Getting everything out on the table always improves the team. I never want to hear a teammate say, "I could have told you that wouldn't work." If you know it beforehand, that's the time to say it.

Besides directness, the other quality team members need to display when communicating with their leaders is respect. Leading a team isn't easy. It takes hard work. It demands personal sacrifice. It requires making tough and sometimes unpopular decisions. We should respect the person who has agreed to take on that role and show him loyalty.

3. Among Teammates

Author Charlie Brower remarked, "Few people are successful unless a lot of other people want them to be." In a team that desires to experience success, all team members must communicate for the common good. That means exhibiting the following qualities:

- *Being supportive.* Former NBA player Earvin "Magic" Johnson summed up support by paraphrasing President John F. Kennedy: "Ask not what your teammates can do for you. Ask what you can do for your teammates." Communication that is focused on giving rather than getting takes the team to a whole new level.

> *"Ask not what your teammates can do for you. Ask what you can do for your teammates."*
>
> —EARVIN "MAGIC" JOHNSON

- *Staying current.* Teammates who rehash old problems and continually open old wounds don't work together. And if they don't work together, they're sunk. As Babe Ruth remarked, "You may have the greatest bunch of individual stars in the world, but if they don't play together, the club won't be worth a dime."

- *Being vulnerable.* Teams are like little communities, and they develop only when the people in them don't posture with one another. In his book *The Different Drum*, psychiatrist M. Scott Peck observes, "If we are to use the word *community* meaningfully, we must restrict it to a group of individuals who have learned how to communicate honestly with each other, whose relationships go deeper than their masks of composure."

Teams succeed or fail based on the way that team members communicate with one another. Martin Luther King Jr. declared, "We must learn to live together as brothers or perish together as fools." If the interaction is strong, then the action teams take can be strong. *Interaction fuels action.* That's the essence of the Law of Communication.

4. Between the Team and the Public

For most teams, communication within the team isn't the only kind that's important. Most teams interact with outsiders in some way, whether the people are clients, customers, or the concerned public. When approached by people from outside the group, team members must remember three Rs; they need to be *receptive, responsive,* and *realistic.* If they receive communication from others gracefully, always respond in a timely fashion, and are realistic about setting and receiving expectations, they will do just fine. Outsiders will perceive that their concerns are being well received.

On the other hand, when it comes to communicating to people who are not on the team, the most important quality a team can display is unity. The more independent team members are, the more difficult that can be; it's not easy to get eagles to fly in formation. Yet the power of unity is incredible.

An old story that I heard when I lived in the Midwest was about a horse-pull at a country fair. That's an event where various horses compete to see which one can pull a sled with the greatest weight. One year, the champion horse pulled 4,500 pounds. The runner-up pulled 4,400. Wondering what the two stout horses might be able to pull together, a group of men yoked them together. They pulled more than 12,000 pounds—an increase of more than 33 percent over their individual efforts.

There's tremendous power in unity. One of the principles I always tell my team is that when we are brainstorming and planning, I want all the ideas and criticisms out on the table. We need an opportunity to hash things out. But once we leave the room, we must be united—even if we face opposition or criticism. We remain a strong team.

When it comes down to it, you spell cooperation "w-e." Working together means winning together. But no team works together unless it's communicating. It takes *interaction to fuel action.* That's just the way it works. That's the Law of Communication.

> *Working together means winning together.*

Hang Together or Hang Separately

One of the most remarkable stories of communication and teamwork I've ever encountered occurred among the U.S. prisoners of war (POWs) who were detained in Vietnam. As American involvement in the war in Vietnam increased, so did the number of U.S. servicemen who were captured. Ultimately 772 servicemen, mostly pilots, were captured and imprisoned.

Most of the prisoners were held at the Hoa Lo prison, which the men called the Hanoi Hilton. There they suffered unspeakable torture and inhumane conditions. Most of them wasted away. It wasn't unusual for someone over six feet tall to weigh 120 pounds. But the worst part for most of the men was the forced solitude. Former POW Ron Bliss explained, "You get isolated. That's when the trouble begins. You have to communicate at virtually any cost. If you get caught and tortured for a little while, that's just the overhead. But you do it anyway."

The North Vietnamese captors at the Hanoi Hilton tried to defeat the POWs by breaking them physically, crushing their spirits, and keeping them isolated. If a man thought of himself as an abandoned individual, then he would give up hope. Jerry Driscoll, a POW who originally thought he might be released after a few months, was told by a fellow prisoner that it might be two years: "When I finally came to that realization that, my God, that's going to be a long time . . . it just kind of hit me all at once. And I just took my blanket and kind of balled it up and I . . . screamed with all this anguish that it's going to be that long. Two years. And when I was finished, I felt, *Oh, okay. I can do that. I can do two years.* Of course, as it turned out, it was two years, and it was two years after that, and two years after that, until it was about seven years in my case."

Taps for the Prisoners

Communication and connection with the other prisoners became necessary for the men to endure and survive. To make that communication possible, the prisoners devised an ingenious system. When four POWs—Carlyle Harris, Phillip Butler, Robert Peel, and Robert Shumaker—were held in the same cell for a time, they devised a tapping code that they could use to spell out words. When they were split up, they used it to communicate, and they taught the code to every prisoner they could. In a matter of months, nearly all of the prisoners knew the code and were using it. "The building sounded like a den of runaway woodpeckers," recalled former POW Ron Bliss.

The men would tap on the walls between cells or push a wire through a wall and tug on it using the code. They would sweep or shovel rhythmically, sending each other messages. They also developed hand signals and other ways of communicating. Ex-POW Thomas McNish observed, "We passed the equivalent of *War and Peace* several times over through different methods of communication."[5]

Even though the prisoners were kept separate from one another—and many men who "talked" all the time never saw the others' faces until they were released—they became a team. They worked together. They shared information. They supported one another. They became such a solid unit that they determined none of them would accept release until all of them could obtain it. The one person who did leave early, Seaman Douglas Hegdahl, accepted release only because he was given a direct order by Lt. Commander Al Stafford to accept it. And he was given the order for one reason: Hegdahl had memorized the 256 names of fellow prisoners, which the men wanted communicated to authorities back home.

Finally in January of 1973, a cease-fire was signed in Paris that made provision for the release of American POWs. They began coming home on February 12, and on March 29, the last prisoners left the

Hanoi Hilton. In all, 462 prisoners were released. That number might have been far fewer if they had not found—and fought for—a way to communicate with one another. But *interaction fuels action.* And their connection with one another fueled their ability to endure and to hold together as a team. That's the value of the Law of Communication.

Teamwork Thought

Communication increases connection.

Becoming a Better Team Member

How committed are you to communicating with the other members of your team? Are you supportive of everyone, even the people who aren't your friends? Are you open and vulnerable, even if it's not pleasant? Are you holding a grudge against anyone on the team? If you are, you need to clear the air. If there are *any* barriers to good communication standing between you and another team member, you need to remove them. That is your responsibility.

Becoming a Better Team Leader

As the leader of an organization, you set the tone for communication. In this chapter, I mention that a leader's communication must be consistent, clear, and courteous. But leaders must also be good listeners. When leaders don't listen . . .

- They stop gaining wisdom.
- They stop "hearing" what isn't being said.
- Team members stop communicating.
- Their indifference spreads to other areas.

Ultimately, poor listening leads to hostility, miscommunication, and a breakdown of team cohesion.

Give yourself a 360-degree review. Ask for feedback concerning your listening skills from your boss or mentor, your colleagues, and your subordinates. If you don't get high marks from all of them, then quiet down, listen up, and work to become a better communicator.

COMPANION ONLINE RESOURCE

Learn more about how the Law of Communication uniquely applies to you.

Take the FREE Law of Communication assessment at **LawsOfTeamwork.com**.

15

THE LAW OF THE EDGE

The Difference Between Two Equally Talented Teams Is Leadership

Teams are always looking for an edge. I'm sure you've seen it. A ball team recruits new talent or develops new plays to beat a tough opponent—or even develops a whole new system to turn around a legacy of losing. Businesses invest in the latest technology, hoping to improve their productivity. Companies fire their ad agencies and hire new ones to launch a campaign, desiring to make gains on major competitors. Corporations cycle through the latest management fads like channel surfers through television reruns. Everyone is seeking the magic formula that will lead to success. The more competitive the field, the more relentless the search.

What is the key to success? Is it talent? Hard work? Technology? Efficiency? To be successful, a team needs all of these things, but it still needs something more. It needs leadership.

- *Personnel* determine the potential of the team.
- *Vision* determines the direction of the team.
- *Work ethic* determines the preparation of the team.
- *Leadership* determines the success of the team.

Everything rises and falls on leadership. If a team has great leadership, then it can gain everything else it needs to go to the highest level.

Finding the Edge

Look at any team that has achieved great success, and you will find that it has strong leadership. What enabled General Electric to gain the respect of the corporate world? The leadership edge of Jack Welch. What sealed the victory of the United States in the Persian Gulf War? The leadership edge of Generals Norman Schwarzkopf and Colin Powell. What powered the Chicago Bulls to win six NBA championships? The leadership edge of Phil Jackson and Michael Jordan. That's why I say *the difference between two equally talented teams is leadership*. That's the Law of the Edge.

> *Look at any team that has achieved great success, and you will find that it has strong leadership.*

To get a clearer picture of the difference that leadership can make, think of the same players on the same team with different leadership. The Los Angeles Lakers are a notable example. During the late 1990s, they struggled despite having a very talented group of players, including Kobe Bryant, who many hoped would be the next Michael Jordan, and Shaquille O'Neal, the best center in the game. Both players were acquired in 1996, yet they continued to have major problems and never clicked as a team. In 1999, teammate Eddie Jones remarked, "Something isn't right with this team. We're all struggling to keep it together and with a team that has that much talent, this shouldn't be going on."[1]

The next year, the team brought in Phil Jackson, the man who had led the Chicago Bulls to six championships, to coach the Lakers. He kept the same team intact with few changes because he knew talent was not the issue. Of his three key players, O'Neal, Bryant, and Glen Rice, Jackson remarked,

> I think we have three of maybe the most talented players since the time of Kareem and Worthy and Magic. However, Baylor, West and Chamberlain [on the 1968–71 Lakers] outshone even those people. They were three of the greatest scorers in the game, and yet they couldn't win a championship. So yeah, we got the talent, we got the show, we got everything else—but how do you make all the pieces complement each other? That's really what my specialty is as a coach, to try to bring that to bear. And this team is learning that.[2]

Leadership is all about understanding players, bringing them together, and getting them to work together as a team to reach their potential. And Jackson provided it. In only one season, the team came together. In 2000, the Lakers won the NBA championship that everyone had believed they had the potential to win. They did it in the same city working under the same conditions and with the same players they'd had in previous years. The only thing that had changed was the leadership. That gave them the edge. *The difference between two equally talented teams is leadership.* That is the Law of the Edge.

Need a Lift?

With good leadership, everything improves. Leaders are lifters. They push the thinking of their teammates beyond old boundaries of creativity. They elevate others' performance, making them better than they've ever been before. They improve their confidence in themselves and each other. And they raise the expectations of everyone on the team. While managers are often able to maintain a team at its current level, leaders are able to lift it to a higher level than it has ever reached before. The key to that is working with people and bringing out the best in them.

- *Leaders transfer ownership for work to those who execute the work.* For a team to succeed, responsibility must go down deep into the organization, down to the roots. Getting that to happen requires a leader who will delegate responsibility and authority to the team. Stephen Covey remarked, "People and organizations don't grow much without delegation and completed staff work, because they are confined to the capacities of the boss and reflect both personal strengths and weaknesses." Good leaders seldom restrict their teams; they release them.

- *Leaders create an environment where each team member wants to be responsible.* Different people require different kinds of motivation to be their best. One needs encouragement. Another needs to be pushed. Another will rise to a big challenge. Good leaders know how to read people and find the key that will make them take responsibility for their part on the team. They also remember that they are responsible *to* their people, not *for* them.

- *Leaders coach the development of personal capabilities.* The team can reach its potential only if each individual on the team reaches his potential. Effective leaders help each player do that. For example, Phil Jackson is well known for giving his players books to read that will help them improve themselves, not just as basketball players, but as people.
- *Leaders learn quickly and encourage others to learn rapidly.* Leaders lift themselves to a higher level first; then they lift the others around them. Modeling comes first, then leadership. If everyone is improving, then the team is improving.

If you want to give a team a lift, then provide it with better leadership. The Law of the Edge works every time.

The Laws of Leadership Impact the Team

Leadership can improve a team and give it an edge in many ways, and the 21 laws from my book on leadership provide a useful summary. Good leaders . . .

1. Do not limit an organization as others do. (The Law of the Lid)
2. Have greater influence than others do. (The Law of Influence)
3. Value the process of developing people more than others do. (The Law of Process)

4. Prepare the team for the journey better than others do. (The Law of Navigation)

5. Communicate more effectively than others do. (The Law of E. F. Hutton)

6. Create momentum and lift the team to a higher level than others do. (The Law of the Big Mo)

7. Stand on a foundation of trust that is more solid than others' is. (The Law of Solid Ground)

8. Command greater respect than others do. (The Law of Respect)

9. Work on leadership issues earlier than others do. (The Law of Intuition)

10. Draw more leaders to themselves than others do. (The Law of Magnetism)

11. Connect with people better than others do. (The Law of Connection)

12. Bring stronger key people around them than others do. (The Law of the Inner Circle)

13. Reproduce more leaders than others do. (The Law of Reproduction)

14. Empower team members more than others do. (The Law of Empowerment)

15. Win with teams more than others do. (The Law of Victory)

16. Sell themselves and their vision to a greater degree than others do. (The Law of Buy-In)

17. Establish priorities more effectively than others do.
    (The Law of Priorities)

18. Understand and use timing more effectively than others do.
    (The Law of Timing)

19. Give up their personal agendas more than others do.
    (The Law of Sacrifice)

20. Grow leaders and organizations faster than others do.
    (The Law of Explosive Growth)

21. Leave a legacy that lasts longer than others do.
    (The Law of Legacy)

Good leaders do things just a little bit better than others do. The result is usually victory. That's the Law of the Edge.

Turning the Table on the Tables

Leadership is the key to the Law of the Edge, but I don't want you to get the idea that the responsibility for leadership always falls on one person. Although most teams have a designated leader who is ultimately responsible for the oversight of the team, the actual leadership of the team is usually shared.

I find that when it comes to leadership, many people tend to see it in one of two ways. The first I call *the myth of the head table.* It's the notion that on a particular team, one person is always in charge in every situation. It's the idea that this particular individual permanently occupies the "head table" in the organization and that everyone else always takes a subordinate role to him. For example, here is an illustration that might have been written by someone who subscribes to the myth of the head table:

> As everyone knows, an executive has practically nothing to do except . . .
> To decide what is to be done;
> To tell somebody to do it;
> To listen to reasons why it should not be done, why it should be done by somebody else, or why it should be done in a different way;
> To follow up to see if the thing has been done, only to discover that it has not;
> To inquire why;
> To listen to excuses from the person who should have done it;
> To follow up again to see if the thing has been done, only to discover that it has been done incorrectly;
> To point out how it should have been done;
> To conclude that as long as it has been done, it may as well be left where it is;
> To wonder if it is not time to get rid of a person who cannot do a thing right;
> To reflect that the person probably has a spouse and large family, and that certainly any successor would be just as bad—or maybe worse;
> To consider how much simpler and better the thing would have been done if one had done it oneself in the first place;
> To reflect sadly that one could have done it right in twenty minutes, and as things turned out, one has had to spend two days to find out why it has taken three weeks for somebody else to do it wrong.

The idea that one person is always doing all the leading is false. The same person should not always lead the team in every situation. The challenge of the moment often determines the leader for that challenge because every person on the team has strengths that come into play. Let me illustrate this point. Even though I lead The INJOY Group as its founder, I don't always lead the team. Other people on the team have gifts, skills, and abilities that I do not possess. When we moved our offices—along with the employees, their equipment, our supplies and computers, our information and communication systems—the job required sophisticated navigating and incredible planning skills.

The most obvious person to lead the team was Frank Hartman, a logistical thinker, exceptional planner, and detailed administrator. Frank created the plan for the move. He had the authority and responsibility of managing the process—and of leading all of the people, including the CEO and other officers of the organization. And he did a wonderful job. We didn't lose a single day of productivity at the office during the move. Nobody else on our team could have pulled it off as effectively. I handed the ball off to Frank, and he successfully led us—and fulfilled the Law of the Edge.

Everyone is important, but everyone isn't equal.

The other misconception about leadership takes the opposite extreme. I call it the *myth of the roundtable.* It's the belief that everyone on the team is equal, all opinions count the same, and a team can function without leadership. That isn't true either. A team that tries to function like a democracy never gets anything done.

Everyone is important, but everyone isn't equal. The person with greater experience, skill, and productivity in a given area is more important to the team in that area. GE CEO Jack Welch's opinion carries more weight than the person who packs boxes on the assembly line. The NBA's Michael Jordan is worth more money than the guard who sits on the bench. That's the way it is. That doesn't mean that Jack and Michael have more value as *human beings.* In the eyes of God, everyone is loved equally. But when it comes to leading the team, somebody needs to step forward.

Giving the Team a Head Start

In essence, leadership is like a running head start for the team. Leaders see farther than their teammates. They see things more quickly than their teammates. They know what's going to happen and can anticipate it. As a result, they get the team moving in the right direction ahead of time, and for that reason, the team is in a position to win. Even an average runner can win a 100-meter race against a world-class sprinter if he has a 50-meter head start.

The greater the challenge, the greater the need for the many advantages that leadership provides. And the more leaders a team develops, the greater the edge from leadership. If you want to win and keep winning for a long time, train players on the team to become better leaders.

The edge gained from good leadership is quite evident in sports, but the power of leadership carries over into every field. The business that is run by a top-notch leader often finds its market niche first and outperforms its rivals, even if the rivals possess greater talent. The nonprofit organization headed by strong leaders recruits more players, equips them to lead, and serves a greater number of people as a result. Even in a technical area such as engineering or construction, leadership is invaluable in ensuring the team is successful.

Golden Opportunity

The Law of the Edge was at work in one of the most extraordinary feats of engineering in the world: the Golden Gate Bridge. Completed in 1937, the bridge had the longest main span of any suspension bridge in the world until the construction of the Verrazano Narrows Bridge was finished in New York City in 1964. If you've been to San Francisco, then you've seen how beautiful and impressive the Golden Gate Bridge is. But the story of its construction is even more impressive.

The concept of a bridge spanning the Golden Gate—the opening to San Francisco's bay—was proposed as early as 1872, although nobody thought it was really possible. The idea wasn't brought up again and taken seriously until 1916. The reason people wanted a bridge was simple: San Francisco's growth and expansion were being hindered by its location since it was surrounded on three sides by water. Plenty of open land lay to the north, but getting to it was hard. Even though Marin County lay only about a mile north across the strait, getting there required a circuitous drive of one hundred miles around San Francisco's huge bay area. The only other alternative was to take a ferry across the gap, but at peak times, drivers had to wait in line for hours to catch the ferry.

Building a bridge across the Golden Gate Strait looked as if it would never happen. The physical and technological challenges of the project were overwhelming. The entrance of the bay experienced strong ocean currents and battering winds. The depth of the channel, which reached more than three hundred feet at points, would make construction very difficult. On top of that, any bridge that would be built had to be high enough to allow large ships to navigate beneath it. Engineers from around the country estimated that a bridge would cost as much as $250 million. (At that time, the value of every piece of property in the entire city of San Francisco totaled only $375 million!)

Enter a Leader

Then along came Joseph B. Strauss. He was the owner of an engineering firm that had built more than four hundred bridges. But more important than his experience were his astonishing vision and powerful leadership. He believed he could build a bridge spanning the Golden Gate for $25 million. In 1921, Strauss put together preliminary designs for a bridge and began to gather support for the project among the leaders of the counties adjoining San Francisco. He promoted the bridge tirelessly. In the beginning, his influence was unofficial. But in time, after the formation of the Golden Gate Bridge and Highway District, he was named chief engineer of the proposed project.

If it hadn't been for a leader like Strauss, the bridge never would have been built. For twelve years, he fought every imaginable obstacle and opponent to the project. When the San Francisco political machine (including the city's chief engineer, Michael O'Shaughnessy) opposed him, he met with leaders and citizens in every county to raise grassroots support. When the Army Corps of Engineers and the War Department (which controlled the land on both sides of the strait) threatened to withdraw approval, Strauss went to Washington and persuaded the secretary of war to guarantee the government's cooperation. When the Golden Gate Bridge and Highway District experienced a severe cash flow problem, Strauss met with Amadeo P. Giannini, founder of Bank of America. In just a few hours he was able to persuade Giannini to buy bonds immediately to keep the project going—

and commit to buy more the next time they were offered. Strauss overcame powerful special interest groups, environmentalists, labor problems, and the ravages of the Great Depression, which hit in the middle of the process. His energy and influence were astounding.

A Leader Who Didn't Get in His Own Way

One of Strauss's greatest strengths was his ability to attract good leaders and engineers. To make the project successful, he brought in the best bridge designers in the world. When he realized that his original design for the bridge was inadequate and could endanger the project, he abandoned it and relied on his leaders to create something better. "Strauss had an unusual ability," remarked author John Van der Zee, "to locate and draw to him men of greater abilities than his own, men who would accept his leadership."[3]

Strauss was a leader's leader, and no matter what difficulty was thrown at him, he handled it. He was a natural leader who understood how to influence others. Van der Zee observed, "Strauss was, if anything, stronger at marketing and promoting ideas than he was at conceiving them. He seemed to know instinctively whom to reach, whom to get to and persuade, who were the decision makers, the people who mattered in any given situation."[4]

Finally Breaking Ground

In 1933, construction finally began on the bridge. Again, Strauss hired the best engineers he could find to oversee construction.

That was no small task. The team who built the bridge put in 25 million hours of work on it.[5] But the actual construction of the bridge seemed almost easy by comparison to what had been necessary before the process could begin. When the bridge was completed, Strauss remarked that it had taken him two decades to convince people that the bridge was feasible, but only four years to actually build it! And he completed it just in time. He died at age sixty-eight—the year after the bridge was finished.

Look behind the scenes of any major undertaking, and you will always find a strong leader. If Joseph Strauss hadn't taken personal responsibility for the creation of the Golden Gate Bridge—and dedicated himself to it wholeheartedly—then it wouldn't have been built. That's the reality of the Law of the Edge. It takes a leader if a team wants to realize its potential and reach its goals. That's why I say that *the difference between two equally talented teams is leadership.*

Teamwork Thought

Everything rises and falls on leadership.

Becoming a Better Team Member

You don't have to be *the* leader to be *a* leader on your team. Begin the process of improving your leadership skills today. Do the following:

- Acknowledge the value of leadership.
- Take personal responsibility for your leadership growth.

- Put yourself on a leadership development program.
- Find a leadership mentor.

Once you have added value to yourself, you will be able to add value to—and influence—others to help your team.

Becoming a Better Team Leader

If you are *the* leader of your team, then the best thing you can do for your teammates is to follow the example of Joseph Strauss. Add other leaders to the team.

You can do that in two ways. First, attract the best leaders you can—people whose talent and potential are greater than your own. Second, develop the people already on the team. The stronger the leadership of the team, the greater the team's potential for success. Never forget: Everything rises and falls on leadership.

COMPANION
ONLINE
RESOURCE

Learn more about how the Law of the Edge uniquely applies to you.

Take the FREE Law of the Edge assessment at **LawsOfTeamwork.com**.

16

THE LAW OF HIGH MORALE

When You're Winning, Nothing Hurts

It's an image most Americans will never forget: gymnast Kerri Strug being carried in the arms of Coach Bela Karolyi to the podium to receive her gold medal along with her six teammates in the 1996 Summer Olympic Games in Atlanta. It was a landmark moment. It was the first time the women's gymnastics team from the United States had won the gold medal, but that isn't why people will remember it. Although it was a stick-in-your-mind image—the tiny eighty-seven-pound Strug being cradled by a big bear of a man who is considered the greatest gymnastics coach in history—it will be remembered primarily because it is the perfect picture of the Law of High Morale.

A First for the Team

Even if you didn't see it on television as I did, you probably know the story. In a sport dominated by the Russian and Romanian teams, the United States team was actually ahead during the Olympic Games. The Russians had opened strong, but after the first rotation of events, the Americans were in first place. As the athletes competed in each event, the U.S. team's lead continued to grow—not by a lot but steadily. As the teams went into the final event—the floor exercise for the Russians and the vault for the Americans—all the U.S. team had to do was to finish solidly, and the gold medal would be theirs.

The second to last vaulter for the U.S. was Dominique Moceanu, usually a smooth performer. Much to everyone's surprise, on her first attempt she landed on her bottom instead of her feet, which gave her a very low score. Fortunately, in women's vault, each athlete gets a second attempt, and only the better of the two scores counts. But, unbelievably, Moceanu missed her second attempt with the same results.

Although Moceanu's performance was unexpected, the situation wasn't desperate. The U.S. still had one athlete left: Kerri Strug, who had received the highest scores in the vault during U.S. Olympic trials. One good vault from her, and the gold medal would belong to the team. When Strug tried to land her first vault, however, her feet weren't positioned quite right. She, too, slipped and fell. Worse yet, she injured herself, and she still needed to complete another vault for the team.

The situation was desperate. After the fact, some commentators remarked that the U.S. could have won without Strug's second vault. But at that moment, Russian gymnast Rozalia Galiyeva was still to compete in the floor exercise. U.S. coach Bela Karolyi was concerned that a high score by the Russian would cost the Americans their hard-fought victory.

Strug knew what she had to do. She needed to land her vault—the final attempt of the final event of the women's team competition. "Give me one last vault," Karolyi encouraged her. "Give me one last good vault."

Not a First for Strug

Every athlete who makes it to the highest levels knows what it means to play through pain. Kerri Strug was no different. Besides all the normal strains, sprains, and bruises, in the past she had recovered from a torn stomach muscle and a serious back injury received in a fall on the uneven parallel bars. Karolyi said of her, "She is just a little girl who was never the roughest girl . . . always a little shy, always standing behind someone else. But sometimes this is the person with the biggest ggrrrrr."[1]

A gymnast has only thirty seconds to complete her second vault after the scores from the first one have been tabulated. In those moments, Strug focused herself. She later remembered, "I knew something was wrong with me. I heard something snap. I kept telling myself not to fall on the vault or the gold would slip away and all that hard work and effort would fall apart in a few seconds. I just said a little prayer and asked God to help me out."[2]

Pain or Gain?

What Strug didn't know then was that two ligaments in her left ankle had torn during her first vault. But that didn't matter. She flew down the runway, hit the beat-board, sprang off the vault with her hands, and went flying through the air. Miraculously, she landed solidly on both feet. Then, she felt excruciating pain. Standing on one foot, she quickly saluted the judges, then crumpled to the floor. She landed her vault, she got her score, and the entire team received its gold medal.

After that, the girl who had always been in the background, who had never been the star of her gym, became the star of the Olympic team. Everyone seemed to appreciate the sacrifice she made. Sports journalist E. M. Swift wrote,

> All she knew, beyond the certainty of the gold medal, was that she had injured herself too badly to compete in the individual all-around competition two days later, a goal she'd clung to for the past four years. This was her moment of greatest triumph, also her moment of greatest disappointment. Her will had found a way to block out the pain for a few crucial seconds, but it had exacted a punishing price. She had literally sacrificed herself for the team.[3]

Strug's own words were direct and simple: "When you do well, you think it's worth it. When you sacrifice so much and you finally do well, it feels really good."[4] In other words, *when you're winning, nothing hurts.* That is the Law of High Morale.

Taking the Team Higher

The Law of High Morale may ring a bell with you because the phrasing of the law was inspired by the words of Joe Namath, the quarterback who helped the New York Jets win the Super Bowl in 1969.

Like any champion, he understood that there is an exhilaration that comes from winning. That feeling can be so strong that it sustains you through the discipline, pain, and sacrifice required to perform at the highest level.

That's what Kerri Strug felt. As she faced that final vault, she knew that her performance would help her team win. And that knowledge empowered her to come through for the team when it mattered most. Perhaps that's why George Allen, who coached the Washington Redskins in the early 1970s, said, "Every time you win, you're reborn; when you lose, you die a little." It's ironic, but if you play hurt, you can put the team in the position to win. And if you win, nothing hurts.

It's ironic, but if you play hurt, you can put the team in the position to win. And if you win, nothing hurts.

Really high morale helps the team to perform at its best. High morale can be a crucial difference maker. When a team has high morale, it doesn't just have to deal with whatever circumstances get thrown at it. It creates its own circumstances.

- The *fund-raiser* knows that under the right circumstances, people love to give.
- The *teacher* knows that under the right circumstances, students love to grow.
- The *leader* knows that under the right circumstances, people love to follow.
- The *coach* knows that under the right circumstances, players are able to win.

High morale is one of the essentials to creating the right circumstances for any team to perform at the highest level.

High Morale Is Great . . .

If the team is winning, then morale is high. And if morale is high, then the team is in a position to win. So which comes first: high morale or winning? I believe that high morale usually comes first. Why? Because high morale magnifies everything positive that is happening for a team.

1. High Morale Is the Great Exaggerator

When an entire team is positive and all the players feel good about themselves, *everything* seems good. Preparation seems to proceed more smoothly. Every break seems to go your way. The small victories seem sweet, and the big ones make you feel almost invincible. The stars of the team deliver at crunch time, and even the bench players seem to be playing beyond their usual capabilities.

Some people call such a time a winning streak or a stretch of good luck. But it's really just high morale. In sports, during times of high morale, everybody jumps onto the bandwagon as a fan. In big business, people buy the company's stock. In entertainment, magazines and television networks ask for interviews—and producers pay top dollar for the team's services. Has the team changed from talentless to talented overnight? Is the team really as good as its press? Probably not. The team is enjoying the great exaggerator at work.

2. High Morale Is the Great Elevator

When a team possesses high morale, the performance of its people goes to a whole new level. The team focuses on its potential, not its problems. Team members become more committed. And everyone finds it easier to be unselfish. Team members are confident, and that confidence helps them to perform at a higher level.

When a team is losing, the opposite effect occurs. Players focus on their problems. Everyone's level of commitment goes down. The team repels others rather than attracts them. And everyone starts to look out for himself rather than his teammates. When you're losing, everything hurts.

3. High Morale Is the Great Energizer

High morale gives a team energy. Players become like the Energizer bunny: They keep going and going. No mountain seems too high. No project seems too difficult. No race seems too long. Their enthusiasm builds along with their energy, and the team develops a momentum that is almost unstoppable.

4. High Morale Is the Great Eliminator

Because of the momentum and energy that come with it, high morale also becomes the great eliminator. While a team that is losing and experiencing poor morale can be hurt by even the most minor problem, a team with high morale will keep right on going even when faced with a huge obstacle or otherwise disabling setback. Problems just seem to disappear—no matter how big they are.

5. High Morale Is the Great Emancipator

Something else that high morale does for a team is to free it up. Winning creates breathing room. A good team with high morale will use that breathing room to take risks and try out new ideas, new moves, new concepts that it otherwise wouldn't. It stops to ask questions that it otherwise might not. And doing these things yields creativity and innovation. In the end, high morale releases the team to reach its potential.

The Four Stages of Morale

You may be saying, "Okay, I agree. *When you're winning, nothing hurts.* High morale is great for the team. How in the world do we get it?" Let me tell you. If you are a player, then you need to have a good attitude, always give your best, and support the people on the team—players and leaders alike. If you have little influence, then exert what influence you have by modeling excellence.

However, if you're one of the team's leaders, then you have more extensive responsibilities. You need to model excellence, but you also need to do more. You need to help the people you lead to develop morale and momentum to create a winning team. The key to knowing what to do can be found in the four stages of morale.

Stage 1: Poor Morale–The Leader Must Do Everything

Nothing is more unpleasant than being on a team when nobody wants to be there. When that is the case, the team is usually negative, feels lethargic, or has no hope. That is often the atmosphere found in a team that is losing.

If you are in that situation, then do the following:

- *Investigate the situation.* Start by addressing what the team is doing wrong. Begin by fixing what's broken. That alone won't give the team high morale, but it will stop giving players reasons to have poor morale.

- *Initiate belief.* A team will change only when people believe in themselves. As the leader, you must initiate that belief. Show people you believe in yourself and them.

- *Create energy.* The desire to change without the energy to change just frustrates people. To bring a greater level of energy to the team, you need to be energetic. Work with energy long enough, and someone on the team will eventually come alongside you and join you. Then another person will. Eventually the energy will spread.

- *Communicate hope.* The deepest need of players at this stage is hope. As Napoleon Bonaparte said, "Leaders are dealers in hope." Help them to see the potential of the team.

> *"Leaders are dealers in hope."*
>
> —NAPOLEON BONAPARTE

In stage one, the only way to get the ball rolling is to start pushing it yourself. As the leader, you can't wait for anyone else to do it.

Stage 2: Low Morale—The Leader Must Do Productive Things

In the beginning, any movement is a noteworthy victory. But to create positive morale, you need to pick up some speed. You need to be productive. After all, you can't steer a parked car! Get the team moving.

- *Model behavior that has a high return.* People do what people see. The best way for them to learn what you expect of them is to model it yourself.

- *Develop relationships with people of potential.* To get any team going in the right direction, you need players who can produce. At this stage, your team may have some producers. If it does, develop relationships with them. If it doesn't, then find the people who have the potential to be productive, and start with them. Don't ask too much of them too soon. Leaders touch a heart before they ask for a hand. That's why you want to begin by building relationships.

- *Set up small victories and talk teammates through them.* Nothing helps people grow in skill and confidence like having some wins under their belts. That's what you want to give the people on your team. Once again, begin with the people who have the most potential. Their small victories will help less talented team members to gain confidence and succeed.

- *Communicate vision.* As I've already explained in the Law of the Compass, vision gives team members direction and confidence. Keep the vision before your team continually.

Once you've got the team really moving, then you can begin to steer.

Stage 3: Moderate Morale—The Leader Must Do Difficult Things

Do you remember what it was like when you first got your driver's license? Maybe before you received it, you enjoyed just sitting in the driver's seat of a car and imagining what it would be like to drive. Later, when you had your license and you were allowed to take out the car, just going for a drive was probably a thrill. It didn't really matter where you went. But as you got older, just driving wasn't enough. Having a destination became significant.

The same is true with a team. Getting the team together and moving add up to an accomplishment. But where you're going matters. To change from simply *moving the team* to *moving the team in the right direction*, you must do the difficult things that help the team to improve and develop high morale. You need to . . .

- *Make changes that make the team better.* You already understand the Law of the Chain. Just remember that leaders are responsible for minimizing the damage any team member can do because of weakness or attitude, and for maximizing the effectiveness of all team members by placing them in their proper niches. Often these actions require tough decisions.

- *Receive the buy-in of team members.* It's one thing to cast vision to the team. It's another to get your teammates to buy in. Yet to build higher morale, you must do that. The teammates must buy into you as a leader, embrace the values and mission of the team, and align themselves with your expectations. If you can do all of that, you will be able to take the team where it needs to go.

- *Communicate commitment.* Part of the process of getting people to buy in comes from showing them your commitment. The Law of Buy-In from *The 21 Irrefutable Laws of Leadership* says that people buy into the leader, then the vision. If you have consistently demonstrated high competence, good character, and strong commitment, you have laid the foundation for your people to buy in.

- *Develop and equip members for success.* Nothing builds morale like success. Most people are not capable of achieving success on their own. They need help, and that is one of the primary reasons for anyone to lead them. If you invest in your teammates, then you help them and the team succeed.

The two toughest stages in the life of the team are the first stage, when you are trying to create movement in a team that's going nowhere, and the third stage, when you must become a change agent. These are the times when leadership is most needed. And stage three is the make-or-break time for a leader. If you can succeed in stage three, then you will be able to create high morale on your team.

Stage 4: High Morale–The Leader Must Do Little Things

In stage four, your job as a leader is to help the team maintain high morale and momentum.

- *Keep the team focused and on course.* High morale leads to winning, and winning maintains morale. That's why it's important to keep team members focused. If they lose focus or get off course, then they'll stop winning. And remember, the farther you intend to go, the greater the impact of an error in direction. If you want to cross a street, being a degree or two off course doesn't hurt you. If you want to cross the ocean, miscalculating by a few degrees can get you into a lot of trouble.

- *Communicate successes.* Knowing what they're doing right helps people stay on track. You can indicate that by communicating the team's successes. Nothing boosts morale like winning and then celebrating it.

- *Remove morale mashers.* Once the team is rolling in the right direction, keep it rolling. The Law of the Big Mo from *The 21*

Irrefutable Laws of Leadership says that momentum is a leader's best friend. Leaders see before others do, so they need to protect the team from the things that will hurt the team.

- *Allow other leaders to lead.* A leader who prepares other team members to lead and then turns them loose to do it accomplishes two things. First, he uses the momentum the team already has to create new leaders for the team. It's easier to make new leaders successful if they are part of a successful team. Second, he increases the leadership of the team. And that makes the team even more successful. A leader who continually does that can create a cycle of success that feeds the team's high morale.

The process of building high morale takes strong leadership, and it takes time. When I think of someone who was a master at that process, I think of Ronald Reagan. When he took office as president of the United States in 1981, morale in the country was at the lowest it had been since the Great Depression. People had lost faith in the American government following Watergate. The threat of nuclear war with the Soviet Union was never far from people's thinking. Inflation was out of control. Oil prices were up. And interest rates were off the charts. People could not have been more discouraged.

Ronald Reagan helped people to

> *Four Stages of Morale:*
> *1. Poor Morale—The leader must do everything.*
> *2. Low Morale—The leader must do productive things.*
> *3. Moderate Morale—The leader must do difficult things.*
> *4. High Morale—The leader must do little things.*

believe in the country again. Under his presidency, the economy revived, the cold war ended, the Berlin Wall fell, and people believed in themselves and their country again.

High Morale at Home

You don't need to have the power of a president or the ability of an Olympic athlete to practice the Law of High Morale. You can apply the principle to your business, your volunteer service, or even your family. In fact, when the Law of High Morale is working at its best, the leader boosts the morale of the team, and the team boosts the morale of the leader. That's the way it should be. *When you're winning, nothing hurts.*

> *When the Law of High Morale is working at its best, the leader boosts the morale of the team, and the team boosts the morale of the leader.*

Let me tell you about a team where the members continually inspire one another and build up one another to such an extent that their morale is high and they keep winning despite the pain they feel. They are the father-and-son team of Dick and Rick Hoyt.

When Rick Hoyt was born in 1962, his parents possessed the typical excited expectations of first-time parents. But then they discovered that during Rick's birth, his umbilical cord had been wrapped around his neck, cutting off the oxygen to his brain. Later, Rick was diagnosed with cerebral palsy. "When he was eight months old," his father, Dick, remembers, "the doctors told us we should put him away—he'd be a vegetable all his life."[5] But Rick's parents wouldn't do that. They were determined to raise him like any other kid.

An Uphill Battle

Sometimes that was tough. Rick is a quadriplegic who cannot speak because he has limited control of his tongue. But Rick's parents worked with him, teaching him everything they could and including him in family activities. When Rick was ten, his life changed; engineers from Tufts University created a device that enabled him to communicate via computer. The first words he slowly and painstakingly punched out were, "Go Bruins." That's when the family, who had been following the NHL's Boston Bruins in the play-offs, found out Rick was a sports fan.

In 1975, after a long battle, the family was finally able to get Rick into public school, where he excelled despite his physical limitations. Rick's world was changing. It changed even more two years later. When Rick found out that a fund-raising 5K race (3.1 miles) was being put on to help a young athlete who had been paralyzed in an accident, he told his father that he wanted to participate.

Dick, a lieutenant colonel in the Air National Guard (who has since retired), was in his late thirties and out of shape. But he agreed to run and push his son in a modified wheelchair. When they crossed the finish line (second to last), Dick recalls, Rick flashed "the biggest smile you ever saw in your life." After the race, Rick wrote out this simple message: "Dad, I felt like I wasn't handicapped." After that day, their lives would never be the same again.

Working Together

What does a father do when his son, who has never been out of a wheelchair, says that he loves to race? He becomes his boy's hands and feet. That's the day "Team Hoyt" was born. Dick got Rick a more sophisticated racing chair. Then the quadriplegic teenager and the out-of-shape dad began running together—and not casually. Before long, they were training seriously, and in 1981, they ran in their first Boston Marathon together. Since then, they haven't missed a Boston Marathon in twenty years.

After four years of running marathons, the two decided that they were ready for another challenge: triathlons, which combine swimming, cycling, and running. That was no small challenge, especially since Dick would have to learn how to swim! But he did. Dick explained, "He's the one who has motivated me because if it wasn't for him, I wouldn't be out there competing. What I'm doing is loaning Rick my arms and legs so he can be out there competing like everybody else."[6]

Of all the races in the world, one is considered the toughest—the Ironman Triathlon in Hawaii. The race consists of three back-to-back legs: a 2.4-mile swim, a 112-mile bike race, and a full marathon run of 26.2 miles. It's an excruciating test of stamina for any individual. In 1989, Dick and Rick competed in the race together. For the swimming portion, Dick towed a small boat with Rick in it. Then he biked for the 112 miles with Rick in a seat on his bicycle's handlebars. By the time they got to the running leg, Dick was exhausted.

But it's in such situations that the Law of High Morale kicks in. All Dick had to do was to think of the words of his son:

> When I'm running, my disability seems to disappear. It is the only place where truly I feel as an equal. Due to all the positive feedback, I do not feel handicapped at all. Rather, I feel that I am the intelligent person that I am with no limits.[7]

When you're winning, nothing hurts. By continuing to run, Dick would be winning for his son, and that's what makes all the training and pain worthwhile. Dick loaded Rick into his running chair, and off they went to finish the Ironman. The pair finished the race in a little over thirteen hours and forty-three minutes—a very strong time.

Since then, Rick has earned his college degree, and he works at Boston University helping to design computer systems for people with disabilities. And of course, he still competes with his father, who is now more than sixty years old. As of March 2001, Team Hoyt had completed a total of 731 races. They had run 53 marathons and 135 triathlons, including 4 races at Ironman distances. And they will keep running. "There is nothing in the world that the both of us can't conquer together," says Dick.[8] He should know. For almost twenty-five years, he and his teammate have been reaping the rewards of the Law of High Morale.

Teamwork Thought

When you do good, you feel good—when you feel good, you do good.

Becoming a Better Team Member

If you want to reap the rewards of the Law of High Morale, you can't wait until your morale is high to begin performing. You need to act your way into feeling, not feel your way into acting. Begin by performing at a level of excellence appropriate for someone who is experiencing a winning season. Your dedication and enthusiasm will help your performance—and will inspire some of your teammates.

Becoming a Better Team Leader

If you are a leader on your team, then you need to figure out what kind of morale your team is currently experiencing:

- *Poor morale:* The team is dead in the water and negative.
- *Low morale:* The team is making some progress, but it is not cohesive and confident.
- *Moderate morale:* The team is experiencing some wins and beginning to believe in itself, but some hard decisions need to be made to take it to the next level.
- *High morale:* The team is performing close to its potential, it's winning, and it just needs to be kept on track.

Once you've determined the stage of your team, then apply the guidelines in the chapter so that you can take the team (or your area of it) to the next stage.

17

THE LAW OF DIVIDENDS

Investing in the Team Compounds Over Time

He's one of the greatest team builders in all of sports, yet you've probably never heard of him. Here is a list of these impressive accomplishments:

- Forty consecutive basketball seasons with at least twenty wins
- Five national championships
- Number one ranking in his region in twenty of the last thirty-three years
- Lifetime winning percentage of .870

His name is Morgan Wootten. And why have most people never heard of him? Because he is a *high school* basketball coach!

When asked to name the greatest basketball coach of all time, most people would respond with one of two names: Red Auerbach or John Wooden. But do you know what John Wooden, the UCLA coach called the Wizard of Westwood, had to say about Morgan Wootten? He was emphatic in his appraisal: "People say Morgan Wootten is the best high school coach in the country. I disagree. I know of no finer coach at any level—high school, college or pro. I've said it elsewhere and I'll say it here: I stand in awe of him."[1]

That's a pretty strong recommendation from the man who won ten NCAA national championships and coached some of the most talented players in the game, including Kareem Abdul-Jabbar. (By the way, when Kareem was in high school at Power Memorial Academy, his team lost only one game—to Morgan Wootten's team!)

No Plan to Be a Team Builder

Morgan Wootten never planned to coach a team. He was a decent athlete in high school, but nothing special. However, he was an excellent talker. When he was growing up, his ambition was to be an attorney. But when he was a nineteen-year-old college student, a friend tricked him into accepting a job coaching baseball, a game he knew little about, to kids from an orphanage. The team had no uniforms and no equipment. And despite working hard, the boys lost all sixteen of their games.

During that first season, Wootten fell in love with those kids. When they asked him to come back and coach football, he couldn't refuse them. Besides, he had played football in high school, so he knew something about it. The orphanage team went undefeated and won the Washington, D.C., Catholic Youth Organization (CYO) championship. But more important, Wootten began to realize that he wanted to invest his time in children, not in court cases.

Even that first year he made a difference in the lives of kids. He remembers one boy in particular who had started stealing and kept being brought back to the orphanage by the police. He described the boy as having "two and a half strikes against him already." Wootten let the boy know he was headed for trouble. But he also took the boy under his wing. Wootten recalled,

> We started spending some time together. I took him to my house and he'd enjoy Mom's meals. He spent weekends with us. He became friends with my brother and sisters. He's still in Washington today and doing quite well and known to a lot of people. Anyone would be proud to call him their son. He was bound for a life of crime and jail, however, and maybe a lot worse, until someone gave him the greatest gift a parent can give a child—his time.

Giving of himself to the people on his teams is something Wootten has done every year since then. NCAA basketball coach Marty Fletcher, a former player and assistant under Wooten, summarized his talent this way: "His secret is that he makes whomever he is with feel like the most important person in the world."[2]

Creating a Dynasty

It wasn't long before Wootten was invited to become an assistant coach at a local powerhouse high school. Then with a couple of years' experience under his belt, he became head coach at DeMatha High School.

When he started at the school in 1956, Wootten was taking over a bunch of losing teams. He called together all of the students who wanted to play sports at DeMatha, and he told them:

> Fellas, things are going to change. I know how bad DeMatha's teams have been during these last few years, but that's over with. We're going to win at DeMatha and we're going to build a *tradition* of winning. Starting right now . . . But let me tell you how we're going to do it. We're going to outwork every team we ever play . . . With a lot of hard work and discipline and dedication, people are going to hear about us and respect us, because DeMatha will be a winner.[3]

That year, the football team won half of its games, which was quite an accomplishment. In basketball and baseball, they were division champions. His teams have been winning ever since. DeMatha has long been considered a dynasty.

On October 13, 2000, Wootten was inducted into the Naismith Basketball Hall of Fame in Springfield, Massachusetts. At that time, his teams had amassed a record of 1,210–183. Over the years, more than 250 of his players have won college scholarships. Twelve players from his high school teams went on to play in the NBA.[4]

It's Not About Basketball

But winning games and honors isn't what excites Wootten most. It's investing in the kids. Wooten says,

> Coaches at every level have a tendency to lose sight of their purpose at times, especially after success arrives. They start to put the cart

> before the horse by working harder and harder to develop their teams, using their boys or girls to do it, gradually forgetting that their real purpose should be to develop the kids, using their teams to do it.[5]

Wootten's attitude reaps rewards not only for the team, but also for the individuals on the team. For example, for a twenty-six-year stretch, every single one of Wootten's seniors earned college scholarships—not just starters but bench players too. Penn State assistant coach Chuck Swenson observed, "Even if you know a kid isn't a great player, if he's a DeMatha player, he'll help your program. With Morgan, you know you're getting a quality kid, who will make good grades and work hard for you."[6] Gary Williams, head coach of the University of Maryland, agreed about the quality of the players: "His players are so fundamentally sound, do so many things right, that they may not improve as much as kids in another program who haven't been as well coached . . . These aren't raw talents: They're refined ones."[7] What's remarkable is that these comments describe *high school* students, not college players or pros.

Investing in the team compounds over time. Morgan Wootten invests in his players because it is the right thing to do, because he cares about them. That practice has made his players good, his teams successful, and his career remarkable. He is the first basketball coach to have won 1,200 games at any level. Developing people pays off in every way. That is the power of the Law of Dividends.

Great Investors

Throughout the chapters of this book, you've read about people who have dedicated themselves to investing in the people on their teams. And those investments pay all kinds of rich dividends. Gordon Bethune's investment of trust has paid off by keeping Continental in business and saving the jobs of its fourteen thousand employees. The investment of Bernie Marcus and Arthur Blank is paying dividends to the employees who own Home Depot stock, including one thousand employee-millionaires. The investment of Jeff Skilling at Enron is paying dividends in the formation of new industry initiatives by leaders in the company. And Lilly Tartikoff's investment in people is paying dividends in cancer research. Usually the time, money, and effort required to develop team members don't change the team overnight, but developing them always pays off. *Investing in the team compounds over time.*

> *The time, money, and effort required to develop team members don't change the team overnight, but developing them always pays off.*

How to Invest in Your Team

I believe that most people recognize that investing in a team brings benefits to everyone on the team. The question for most people isn't *why,* but *how.* Allow me to share with you ten steps you can take to invest in your team. You can implement these practices whether you are a player or coach, employee or employer, follower or leader. There is always someone on the team who can benefit from what you have to offer. And when everyone on the team is investing, then the benefits are like those of compound interest. They multiply.

Here is how to get started:

1. Make the Decision to Build a Team . . . This Starts the Investment in the Team

It's said that every journey begins with the first step. Deciding that people on the team are worth developing is the first step in building a better team. That requires *commitment.*

> *Deciding that people on the team are worth developing is the first step in building a better team.*

2. Gather the Best Team Possible . . . This Elevates the Potential of the Team

As I've previously mentioned, the better the people on the team, the greater the potential. There's only one kind of team that you may be a part of where you *shouldn't* go out and find the best players available, and that's family. You need to stick with those teammates through thick and thin. But every other kind of team can benefit from the recruitment of the very best people available.

3. Pay the Price to Develop the Team . . . This Ensures the Growth of the Team

When Morgan Wootten extended himself to benefit the kid who had two-and-a-half strikes against him, he and his family had to pay a price to help that boy. It wasn't convenient or comfortable. It cost them in energy, money, and time.

It will cost you to develop your team. You will have to dedicate time that could be used for personal productivity. You will have to spend money that could be used for personal benefit. And sometimes you will have to set aside your personal agenda. But the benefit to the individuals—and the team—is worth the price. Everything you give is an investment.

4. Do Things Together as a Team . . . This Provides Community for the Team

I once read the statement, "Even when you've played the game of your life, it's the feeling of teamwork that you'll remember. You'll forget the plays, the shots, and the scores, but you'll never forget your teammates." That is describing the community that develops among teammates who spend time doing things together.

> *Even when you've played the game of your life, it's the feeling of teamwork that you'll remember.*

The only way to develop community and cohesiveness among your teammates is to get them together, not just in a professional setting but in personal ones as well. There are lots of ways to get yourself connected with your teammates, and to connect them with one another. Many families who want to bond find that camping does the trick. Business colleagues can socialize outside work (in an appropriate way). The *where* and *when* are not as important as the fact that team members share common experiences.

5. Empower Team Members with Responsibility and Authority . . . This Raises Up Leaders for the Team

The greatest growth for people often occurs as a result of the trial and error of personal experience. Any team that wants people to step up to a higher level of performance—and to higher levels of leadership—must give team members authority as well as responsibility. If you are a leader on your team, don't protect your position or hoard your power. Give it away. That's the only way to empower your team.

6. Give Credit for Success to the Team . . . This Lifts the Morale of the Team

Mark Twain said, "I can live for two months on one good compliment." That's the way most people feel. They are willing to work hard if they receive recognition for their efforts. That's why Napoleon Bonaparte observed, "A soldier will fight long and hard for a bit of colored ribbon." Compliment your teammates. Talk up their accomplishments. And if you're the leader, take the blame but never the credit. Do that and your team will always fight for you.

> *"I can live for two months on one good compliment."*
>
> —MARK TWAIN

7. Watch to See That the Investment in the Team Is Paying Off . . . This Brings Accountability to the Team

If you put money into an investment, you expect a return—maybe not right away, but certainly over time. How will you know whether you are gaining or losing ground on that investment? You have to pay attention to it and measure its progress.

The same is true of an investment in people. You need to observe whether you are getting a return for the time, energy, and resources you are putting into them. Some people develop quickly. Others are slower to respond, and that's okay. The main outcome you want to see is progress.

8. Stop Your Investment in Players Who Do Not Grow . . . This Eliminates Greater Losses for the Team

One of the most difficult experiences for any team member is leaving a teammate behind. Yet that is what you must do if someone on your team refuses to grow or change for the benefit of teammates. As I mentioned in the Law of the Chain, that doesn't mean that you love the person less. It just means you stop spending your time trying to invest in someone who won't or can't make the team better.

9. Create New Opportunities for the Team . . . This Allows the Team to Stretch

There is no greater investment you can make in a team than giving it new opportunities. When a team has the possibility of taking new ground or facing new challenges, it has to stretch to meet them. That process not only gives the team a chance to grow, but it also benefits every individual. Everyone has the opportunity to grow toward his or her potential.

10. Give the Team the Best Possible Chance to Succeed . . . This Guarantees the Team a High Return

James E. Hunton says, "Coming together is a beginning. Keeping together is progress. Working together is success." One of the most essential tasks you can undertake is to clear obstacles so that the team has the best possible chance to work toward success. If you are a team member, that may mean making a personal sacrifice or helping others to work together better. If you are a leader, that means creating an energized environment for the team and giving each person what he needs at any given time to ensure success.

Where there's a will there's a way; where there's a team, there's more than one way.

Investing in a team almost guarantees a high return for the effort because a team can do so much more than individuals. Or as Rex Murphy, one of my conference attendees, told me: "Where there's a will there's a way; where there's a team, there's more than one way."

My Personal Investment—and Return

Once you have experienced what it means to invest in your team, you will never be able to stop. Thinking about my team—about how the teammates add value to me as I add value to them—brings me abundant joy. And just like my investment and their return, my joy continues to compound.

I value everyone on my team, and if I could, I would tell you about every person. But since that isn't possible, I want to at least acquaint you with key players in my inner circle:

- Larry Maxwell (fifty-four years). He loves me unconditionally. He has taken The INJOY Group to a whole new level. Asks great questions. Keeps our team focused. Protects me. He's my big brother!
- Margaret Maxwell (thirty-seven years). My wife. She knows me so well, loves me so much. Her partnership has allowed me to go to a higher level. Our journey together is my greatest joy.
- Dan Reiland (nineteen years). He was my executive pastor for many years. Now as a consultant, he helps pastors with my heart and experience plus his wisdom and perspective. He is a pastor's best friend and mine!
- Dick Peterson (eighteen years). He follows up on all the details of my company. I open the door, and he closes it. I start a sentence, and he finishes it!

- Tim Elmore (fifteen years). He teaches my leadership material better than I do. He gives me leadership material better than my own.
- Linda Eggers (fourteen years). She knows my strengths and weaknesses. Represents me so well. Answers the team's questions better than I would and much more quickly.
- Charlie Wetzel (eight years). He shapes the lives of more people than anyone else on my team. He takes my ideas, lessons, and outlines and turns them into books. From there, they multiply.
- Dave Johnson (seven years). He stewards The INJOY Group's resources to extend its impact around the globe. He is a financial wizard who loves and understands me.
- Kevin Small (seven years). He has unlimited energy and unlimited potential. Sees an opportunity a mile away. I love pouring myself into him. The return is huge!
- Dave Sutherland (seven years). He is my number one guy. He's the man. A great thinker. He can grow the company without me. When I give him the ball, it's always a touchdown.
- Kirk Nowery (five years). He represents me so well and loves pastors and local churches. Every night he tells the story of how we can add value through ISS. Every night we get that opportunity.
- Doug Carter (five years). He loves to share the mission of EQUIP (my nonprofit organization) with others. He helps businesspeople go from success to significance. He has taken me to a whole new level.

At this stage of my life, everything I do is a team effort. When I first started teaching seminars, I did everything. Certainly there were other people pitching in, but I was just as likely to pack and ship a box as I was to speak. Now, I show up and teach. My wonderful team takes care of everything else. Even the book you're reading was a team effort.

My team is my joy. I would do anything for the people on my team because they do everything for me:

> My team makes me better than I am.
> My team multiplies my value to others.
> My team enables me to do what I do best.
> My team gives me more time.
> My team represents me where I cannot go.
> My team provides community for our enjoyment.
> My team fulfills the desires of my heart.

If your current team experiences are not as positive as you would like, then it's time to increase your level of investment. Building a team for the future is just like developing a financial nest egg. It may start slowly, but what you put in brings a high return—similar to the way that compound interest works with finances. Try it and you will find that the Law of Dividends really works. *Investing in the team compounds over time.*

Teamwork Thought

Is the team's investment in you paying off?

Becoming a Better Team Member

Are you giving a good return for what your teammates are investing in you? Think about the opportunities you have received and the positive learning experiences to which you've been exposed. Have you seized all of them enthusiastically, or have you allowed many of them to slip by?

If you've been lackadaisical about pursuing growth opportunities, then change your attitude today. Grow all you can, and determine to give the team a good return on its investment in you.

Becoming a Better Team Leader

As a leader, you, more than anyone else, determine the environment of your organization and whether your people are investing in others. Begin by institutionalizing investment and making it a part of your organization's culture. Encourage growth. Set aside time and money for investment in the team. And take on the responsibility for investing in your core leaders. The more leaders you have on the team and the further developed they are, the greater the dividends.

COMPANION ONLINE RESOURCE

Learn more about how the Law of Dividends uniquely applies to you.

Take the FREE Law of Dividends assessment at **LawsOfTeamwork.com**.

AFTERWORD

A lot of people talk about team chemistry. You hear it often in sports. Analysts will say, "That team certainly had the talent, but they weren't able to develop the chemistry. That's why they didn't perform the way everyone expected."

You may have noticed that there is no Law of Chemistry in this book, and that may have been a disappointment to you. But let me tell you why that concept isn't one of the 17 Indisputable Laws of Teamwork.

Chemistry isn't something you can create with one skill or implementation of a single technique. Chemistry develops when you are able to implement *all* of the Laws of Teamwork. The more laws you put into practice, the greater the chemistry your team will develop. Each time a player finds his niche on the team, it helps to create positive chemistry. Each time a weak link is replaced by a better player from the bench, it creates better chemistry. When a catalyst steps up to the plate and makes something happen for the first time, or when a leader finds a way to help the team perform at a higher level, it creates good chemistry. When players finally count on one another, it makes the chemistry better. Every time another law comes to life for the team, the chemistry gets that much better—and the team gets that much stronger.

I hope you have enjoyed learning about the Laws of Teamwork. More important, I hope they will help you develop the team of your dreams. Embrace them and you will empower your team. That is my promise to you!

NOTES

Chapter 1

1. Brandon Tartikoff and Charles Leerhsen, *The Last Great Ride* (New York: Turtle Bay Books, 1992), 60.
2. "OncoLink: An Interview with Lilly Tartikoff," <www.oncolink.upenn.edu>.

Chapter 2

1. Frye Gaillard, *If I Were a Carpenter: Twenty Years of Habitat for Humanity* (Winston-Salem, NC: John F. Blair, 1995).
2. "The History of Habitat," <www.habitat.org>.

Chapter 3

1. "Bush Nominates Powell as Secretary of State," 17 December 2000.
2. Colin Powell with Joseph E. Persico, *My American Journey* (New York: Random House, 1995), 28.

3. Michael Hirsh and John Barry, "Leader of the Pack," *Newsweek* <www.newsweek.com>, 25 December 2000.
4. "Town Hall Meeting: January 25, 2001," <www.state.gov>.
5. "Packing Parachutes," audiotape excerpt, <www.charlieplumb.com>.
6. "Charlie Plumb's Speech Content," <www.charlieplumb.com>.

Chapter 4

1. "Mount Everest History/Facts," <www.mnteverest.com>.
2. James Ramsey Ullman, *Man of Everest: The Autobiography of Tenzing* (London: George G. Harrap and Co., 1955), 178.
3. Ibid., 250.
4. Ibid., 255.
5. Jim Lovell and Jeffrey Kluger, *Lost Moon: The Perilous Voyage of Apollo 13* (Boston: Houghton Mifflin, 1994), 159–60.
6. W. David Compton, *Where No Man Has Gone Before: A History of Apollo Lunar Exploration Missions* (Washington DC: NASA SP-4214, 1989).
7. Ullman, *Man of Everest*, 227.

Chapter 5

1. "Quick Answers to the Most Frequently Asked Questions," <www.oilspill.state.ak.us/history>.
2. "Exxon's Appeal of the Valdez Oil Spill $5 Billion in Punitive Judgement," <www.exxon.mobil.com>.
3. Danny Cox with John Hoover, *Leadership When the Heat's On* (New York: McGraw-Hill, 1992), 69–70.
4. John Carl Roat, *Class-29: The Making of U.S. Navy SEALs* (New York: Ballantine Books, 1998), 192.

5. Ibid., 7.
6. Ibid., 223.

Chapter 6

1. "The President Suits Up for Practice," <www.cbs.sportsline.com>.
2. "The History of the 'I Have a Dream' Program," <www.ihad.org>.

Chapter 7

1. Greg Farrell, "Building a New Big Blue," <www.usatoday.com>, 23 November 1999.
2. "IBM Wants Business Partners to Focus on Growth," <www.findarticles.com>, 2 March 1999.
3. Farrell, "Building a New Big Blue."
4. Michelle Marchetti, "IBM's Marketing Visionary," *Sales and Marketing Management,* September 2000, 55.
5. Proverbs 29:18 KJV.
6. Howard Schultz and Dori Jones Yang, *Pour Your Heart into It: How Starbucks Built a Company One Cup at a Time,* (New York: Hyperion, 1997), 36-37.
7. Ibid., 3-4.
8. Ibid., 102.
9. Ibid., 101.
10. Alex Frew McMillan, "Starbucks' Schultz on Being Big in Japan," <www.cnn.com>, 10 October 2001.
11. "Howard Schultz," *BusinessWeek,* <www.businessweek.com>, 14 January 2002.
12. Schultz and Jones Yang, 200.

Chapter 8

1. John C. Maxwell, *The Winning Attitude* (Nashville: Thomas Nelson, 1993), 24.
2. Pat Riley, *The Winner Within* (New York: Berkley Publishing Group, 1994), 41, 52.

Chapter 9

1. "Interview with Stacey Loizeaux."
2. John C. Maxwell, *The 21 Irrefutable Laws of Leadership: Follow Them and People Will Follow You* (Nashville: Thomas Nelson, 1998), 58.
3. Barry J. Gibbons, *This Indecision Is Final: 32 Management Secrets of Albert Einstein, Billie Holiday, and a Bunch of Other People Who Never Worked 9 to 5* (Chicago: Irwin Professional Publishing, 1996).
4. Colossians 3:23–24.
5. Roat, *Class-29: The Making of U.S. Navy SEALs*, 135–36.
6. "Statement of FBI Director Louis J. Freeh on the Arrest of FBI Special Agent Robert Philip Hanssen," <www.fbi.gov>, 20 February 2001.
7. Walter Pincus and Brooke A. Masters, "U.S. May Seek Death Penalty Against Accused Spy Hanssen," <www.washingtonpost.com>, 28 March 2001.
8. "Core Values," <www.fbi.gov>, 30 March 2001.
9. "Statement of FBI Director Louis J. Freeh on the Arrest of FBI Special Agent Robert Philip Hanssen."
10. William A. Cohen, *The Art of the Leader* (Englewood Cliffs, NJ: Prentice Hall, 1994).

Chapter 10

1. Stephen Franklin, "Founder a Force in Retail, Civic Affairs," <www.chicagotribune.com>, 29 December 2000.

2. "End of the Line," <www.nytimes.com>, 29 December 2000.
3. "Historical Chronology—1925: Opening Retail Stores," <www.sears.com>, 15 March 2001.
4. Allan Cox, *Straight Talk for Monday Morning* (New York: John Wiley & Sons, 1990).
5. John C. Maxwell, *The 21 Indispensable Qualities of a Leader: Becoming the Person Others Will Want to Follow* (Nashville: Thomas Nelson, 1999), 144–45.
6. Robert Newall, "History Comes Alive in Valley Forge," <www.vaportrails.com>, 11 March 2001.

Chapter 11

1. Michael D. Eisner with Tony Schwartz, *Work in Progress* (New York: Random House, 1998), 171.
2. John Taylor, *Storming the Magic Kingdom: Wall Street Raiders and the Battle for Disney* (New York: Knopf, 1987), 14.
3. Eisner, *Work in Progress,* 235.
4. "The Walt Disney Company Annual Report 2000: Financial Review," <www.disney.go.com>, 28 March 2001.
5. Adam Cohen, "eBay's Bid to Conquer All," *Time,* 5 February 2001, 48.
6. "Company Overview," <pages.ebay.com>, 12 March 2001.

Chapter 12

1. John Wooden with Jack Tobin, *They Call Me Coach* (Chicago: Contemporary Books, 1988), 104.

Chapter 13

1. Bernie Marcus and Arthur Blank with Bob Andelman, *Built from Scratch: How a Couple of Regular Guys Grew The Home Depot*

from Nothing to $30 Billion (New York: Times Business, 1999), xvi–xvii.

2. "Company Information," <www.homedepot.com>, 11 April 2001.
3. Marcus and Blank, *Built from Scratch,* xvii.

Chapter 14

1. Gordon Bethune with Scott Huler, *From Worst to First: Behind the Scenes of Continental's Remarkable Comeback* (New York: John Wiley and Sons, 1998), 4.
2. Ibid., 6.
3. Thomas A. Stewart, "Just Think: No Permission Needed," *Fortune,* 8 January 2001, <www.fortune.com>.
4. Bethune, *From Worst to First,* 211.
5. "Return with Honor," *The American Experience,* <www.pbs.org>, 22 February 2001.

Chapter 15

1. Mike Kahn, "Harris' Deletion No Surprise," <www.cbs.sportsline.com>, 24 February 1999.
2. Mike Rowland, *Los Angeles Magazine,* June 2000, <www.findarticles.com>.
3. John Van der Zee, *The Gate: The True Story of the Design and Construction of the Golden Gate Bridge* (Lincoln, NE: Backinprint.com, 2000), 50.
4. Ibid., 42.
5. Craig A. Doherty and Katherine M. Doherty, *The Golden Gate Bridge* (Woodbridge, CT: Blackbirch Press, 1995), 17.

Chapter 16

1. Johnette Howard, "True Grit," <sportsillustrated.cnn.com>, 24 July 1996.
2. Ibid.
3. E. M. Swift, "Carried Away with Emotion," <sportsillustrated.cnn.com>, 8 December 1996.
4. "Not Just the Wink of an Eye," <www.strug.com>, 30 March 2001.
5. David Tereshchuk, "Racing Towards Inclusion," <www.teamhoyt.com>, 14 March 2001.
6. "Father-Son Duo Are World Class Competitors, Despite Odds," <www.cnn.com>, 29 November 1999.
7. Ibid.
8. Ibid.

Chapter 17

1. Don Banks, "Teacher First, Seldom Second, Wootten has Built Monument to Excellence at Maryland's DeMatha High," *St. Petersburg Times*, 3 April 1987, <www.dematha.org>.
2. John Feinstein, "A Down-to-Earth Coach Brings DeMatha to New Heights," *Washington Post*, 27 February 1984, <www.dematha.org>.
3. Morgan Wootten and Bill Gilbert, *From Orphans to Champions: The Story of DeMatha's Morgan Wootten* (New York: Atheneum, 1979), 24–25.
4. William Plummer, "Wooten's Way," *People*, 20 November 2000, 166.
5. Wootten and Gilbert, *From Orphans to Champions*, 12–13.
6. Feinstein, "A Down-to-Earth Coach Brings DeMatha to New Heights."
7. Ibid.

The INJOY Group™
A Lifelong Partner Dedicated to Lifting Your Potential

The INJOY Group™, founded in 1985 by Dr. John C. Maxwell, dedicates itself to adding value to individuals and organizations across America and around the world. It accomplishes its mission by forging lasting partnerships that foster personal growth and organizational effectiveness.

The INJOY Group™ consists of . . .

INJOY® Resources—Equipping People to Succeed

INJOY® Conferences—Empowering Leaders to Excel

INJOY Stewardship Services®—Energizing Churches to Raise Funds for Financing the Future

EQUIP™—Affecting Leadership Development in Emerging Countries, American Urban Centers, and Academic Communities

Each year, The INJOY Group™ partners with tens of thousands of people, dozens of church denominations, and countless business and non-profit organizations to help people reach their potential.

To learn more about Dr. John C. Maxwell or any division of The INJOY Group™, visit us at:

www.INJOY.com

Books by Dr. John C. Maxwell Can Teach You How to Be a REAL Success

Relationships

Be a People Person (Victor Books)
Becoming a Person of Influence (Thomas Nelson)
The Power of Influence (Honor Books)
The Power of Partnership in the Church (J. Countryman)
The Treasure of a Friend (J. Countryman)

Equipping

Developing the Leaders Around You (Thomas Nelson)
Partners in Prayer (Thomas Nelson)
The Success Journey (Thomas Nelson)
Success One Day at a Time (J. Countryman)

Attitude

Be All You Can Be (Victor Books)
Failing Forward (Thomas Nelson)
The Power of Thinking (Honor Books)
Living at the Next Level (Thomas Nelson)
Think On These Things (Beacon Hill)
The Winning Attitude (Thomas Nelson)
Your Bridge to a Better Future (Thomas Nelson)
The Power of Attitude (Honor Books)

Leadership

The 21 Indispensable Qualities of a Leader (Thomas Nelson)
The 21 Irrefutable Laws of Leadership (Thomas Nelson)
The 21 Most Powerful Minutes in a Leader's Day (Thomas Nelson)
Developing the Leader Within You (Thomas Nelson)
The Power of Leadership (Honor Books)
The 17 Indisputable Laws of Teamwork (Thomas Nelson)
The 17 Essential Qualities of a Team Player (Thomas Nelson, Jan. 2002)

1160 (07126)